· A HISTORY LOVER'S ·
GUIDE TO
LEXINGTON &
CENTRAL KENTUCKY

FOSTER OCKERMAN JR. & PETER BRACKNEY

THE
History
PRESS

Published by The History Press
Charleston, SC
www.historypress.com

First published 2020

Manufactured in the United States

ISBN 9781467142991

Library of Congress Control Number: 2020938496

Notice: The information in this book is true and complete to the best of our knowledge. It is offered without guarantee on the part of the authors or The History Press. The authors and The History Press disclaim all liability in connection with the use of this book.

CONTENTS

AUTHORS' NOTE

History cannot be changed. What has happened in the past cannot be altered. However, it can be understood differently or more completely depending on the lens we use or newly discovered information. The view of events and people making history can be reinterpreted based on changing social mores and the contemporary understanding of justice.

In the early twentieth century, many Kentuckians interpreted the Civil War and slavery through a lens that romanticized the South's Lost Cause. Today, society is properly recognizing the error in that interpretation. A changed understanding of the history of our nation, state, and region has resulted in the names of places being altered and certain memorials to the past being removed, relocated, or altered. This is not a loss of history; it is a retelling of history through a modern interpretation. This is not the first time such changes have been made in Lexington. As noted Kentucky historian Dr. Patrick Lewis, scholar in residence at the Filson Society, has observed with regard to statues, but equally applicable to site names: "Their construction was a political decision. Their removal is a political decision."

In 2017, Lexington relocated two large statues of Confederates from the old courthouse lawn to the Lexington Cemetery. One of those statues was located in Cheapside Park. We reference Cheapside and explain the origin of that name (after a London, England market district) as well as highlight that it was in Cheapside Park where slaves were sold, both on the courthouse steps pursuant to court order and in private brokerage houses nearby. While final editing of this book was in process, Lexington mayor Linda Gorton announced plans to rename Cheapside Park as the Henry A. Tandy Centennial Park. Tandy was a freed slave who formed a successful masonry company in Lexington, Tandy & Byrd, which did the masonry work on construction of the old courthouse overlooking the park.

A few short days before the mayor's announcement, faculty from the University of Kentucky's African American and Africana Studies program called for Rupp Arena to be renamed. Opened in 1976, Rupp Arena is named after Coach Adolph Rupp, who coached the university's men's basketball program from 1930 until 1972 while leading the program to greatness and winning four national championships. Despite his success on the basketball court, the AAAS faculty assert that the Rupp name "has come to stand for racism." As of this writing, it is unclear whether the basketball facility will be renamed.

Faced with our publisher's deadline approaching faster than community decision making, we chose to use the names historically and presently associated with these places. Other name changes and even physical relocations could be forthcoming—indeed, may be predictable.

Foster Ockerman Jr.

Peter Brackney

1

A CONCISE HISTORY OF LEXINGTON AND THE BLUEGRASS

What the colonists called the French and Indian War ended with the Treaty of Paris in 1763. The conflict was known among the major powers in Europe as the Seven Year's War.

According to the terms of the treaty, France surrendered its claims in North America to England for lands east of the Mississippi River, and to Spain for those to the west. England's King George III immediately drew a Line of Demarcation along the crests of the Allegheny Mountains intending to prohibit any of his subjects along the Atlantic coast from crossing the mountains. His reasons were partly economic (the war had been expensive and he didn't want to incur any more military costs), partly political (the various colonies had conflicting claims to the western lands), and partly strategic (to divert expansion of the colonial population north toward Nova Scotia and south toward Florida along the Atlantic coast). That, of course, did not deter adventurous men from probing the mountain ranges, looking for a way through the mountains.

This chapter explores the history of central Kentucky from its earliest peoples to the twenty-first century, from buffalo traces and Indian war paths to interstates. The precolonial history of Native Americans in the region, in particular, is rich and deep and not often explored in popular histories. It leads to conflicts with the frontiersmen breaking through the Allegheny Mountains, to colonial wars, and, with independence and statehood, the growth of Lexington and the other settlements in central Kentucky.

Two particular myths need to be debunked first, however dear these myths may be to the hearts of Kentucky children who were taught them: (1) the word *Kentucky* is not "Indian" for "dark and bloody ground" and (2) no tribes ever lived in Kentucky; they only hunted and fought there. There was and is, of course, no singular Native American language, and several tribes were active in Kentucky and Tennessee during our frontier period. In March 1775, Daniel Boone and others acting for the Transylvania Company were negotiating with the Chickamauga Cherokee tribal leaders to purchase a large area of land comprising what is now the central and eastern parts of Kentucky and Tennessee. One leader, Chief Dragging Canoe, opposed the sale. He threatened to make the land a "dark and bloody ground" if any White people attempted to settle there and left the conference. A treaty was eventually concluded, but it was negated by the legislatures of Virginia and North Carolina, which claimed the land. That Native Americans who lived in Kentucky are described in the following sections.

The true original meaning of *Kentucky* in its various spellings has not been determined, but a strong contender is the Iroquois word *kentaki*, which means "place of level land" or "place of meadows." It is believed to have been the place name for where the Iroquois village of Eskippakithiki was located in the southeast corner of present-day Clark County to the east of Lexington. Daniel Boone and other early adventurers picked up the name and applied it more generally to the rolling lands of the Bluegrass Region, certainly full of meadows and level compared to the mountains down which they had climbed.

PRE-COLUMBIAN

The first peoples entered what is now Kentucky more than 11,500 years ago. The Clovis people, known for their distinctive spear points, were first. Their points featured fluted, chipped rock heads. The Clovis were hunter-gatherers living in extended family groups of one to two dozen and moved across the area. They hunted the megafauna of the time, mastodons and mammoths, as well as smaller game. Related family groups formed loose economic and social ties. Their period ended roughly 8000 BCE.

ARCHAIC

For the next two thousand years, the Archaic peoples lived in Kentucky. Like their ancestors, they were nomads and hunter-gatherers, but the nature of the game they hunted had changed. They also began experimenting with growing their own crops, as some groups began to make camps by streams and in caves. Axes appeared at this time, as did woven baskets, mats, and fishnets.

WOODLAND PERIOD

The Adena culture, which lasted from roughly 500 BCE to 200 CE, found family groups clustering into clans and building semipermanent settlements. The hunters did move seasonally to follow game, but farming or gardening was more prevalent. They also maintained extended relations and trading routes with other tribes. Famously, the Adena built burial mounds for certain of their dead, believed to have been important political, war, or religious leaders. The Adena also used herbal medicines to treat maladies and made pottery tempered with native limestone and sometimes decorated with geometric designs.

FORT ANCIENT PEOPLES

The Fort Ancient period stretched from 900 CE to 1750 CE, chiefly in central and eastern Kentucky. While still engaged in hunting game and gathering native plants, the Fort Ancient built permanent villages. The earlier villages tended to be a ring of small houses around a center plaza. Storage pits were next to each house. After about 1400, the villages grew in size. Some of these villages housed up to five hundred people. Their arrows were now tipped with flint heads, and other tools such as scrapers, knives, and drills were made from a strong, dark rock called chert. Potters made an extensive variety of bowls, pitchers, and jars. Personal ornaments of bone and shell were frequent. The old trading networks had been extended; not long after the early 1600s settlements at Jamestown and Plymouth, metal objects of European origin began filter into these villages.

HISTORIC PERIOD

The historic period in Kentucky is generally considered to begin in 1750 with the discovery of the Cumberland Gap in the mountains by Dr. Thomas Walker, which marked the first relatively easy route from Virginia into the area. (Native Americans, of course, had long be aware of the Gap.) The Wilderness Road was blazed from the Cumberland Gap into central Kentucky to end at present-day Danville. The Limestone Road, named for a settlement on the Ohio River (present-day Maysville) led south toward what became Lexington. (Limestone Street, a north–south axis through Lexington's downtown, takes its name from this road.) As the English settlers began to infiltrate Kentucky, several tribes lived in parts of Kentucky and defended against the intrusions. The Shawnee lived and hunted in central Kentucky, maintaining a string of villages along the Kentucky side of the Ohio River. They were the most prominent players in opposing the colonists. The Chickasaw fought to retain western Kentucky, while the Chickamauga Cherokee defended their lands in south-central Kentucky and Tennessee. The Miami, Mingo, and Wyandot tribes also fought in the war for Kentucky. During the French and Indian War, both the English and the French enlisted Native Americans to fight. During the Revolutionary War, the British from their bases in Canada would stir up tribes to attack the growing Kentucky settlements. Again, in the War of 1812, England mounted attacks into Kentucky leading Native American forces. In between those wars, the tribes made life unsettling for the new arrivals.

The last Native American settlement of any significance was the village of Eskippakithiki in the southeast corner of modern-day Clark County, where the Bluegrass Region gives rise to the mountains of Eastern Kentucky. The Iroquois tribe, which settled there in roughly 1718, called the area *kentaki* or "land of meadows." The name would be attached to the nearby river and eventually the entire state. The village name itself means "place of blue licks," in reference to the salt licks in the area. A salt or mineral lick is an exposed deposit of salt and other minerals needed by animals. They would literally lick the ground to get the salt and made trails from one lick to another. Indians and frontiersmen easily followed these paths to hunt the animals, so it was natural for a settlement to be made near both the licks and the Kentucky River. A French census in 1736, when that nation still claimed the area, found two hundred men lived in the village. That census counted only heads of households, so the population could have been five to eight hundred or more once women and children were included. The village was attacked in 1754 by a war party from the Ottowa tribe and appears to have been abandoned shortly thereafter. The Iroquois are believed to have traveled north to join a string of Iroquois settlements along the Ohio River in southern Ohio.

Various tribes continued to hunt in Kentucky, but the age of residence in Kentucky was almost over.

SOME SPECIFIC INSTANCES OF ATTACKS

On December 22, 1769, Daniel Boone and members of his hunting party were attacked and captured by members of the Shawnee tribe. After taking their furs and supplies, the Native Americans released the men with the warning never to return or "the wasps and yellow jackets would sting them." The threat had little effect; Boone and his men stayed in the area. They were soon captured again but escaped.

In 1771, Boone and his hunters were attacked and robbed by Cherokee. Later in the year, Boone had several encounters with Native Americans.

In 1776, as revolution and independence were declared along the Atlantic coast colonies, a very different struggle existed in central Kentucky. In April, the small village of Leestown, near present-day Frankfort on the Kentucky River, was attacked. The survivors abandoned the village and fled to Fort Harrod. In May, Boonesboro was attacked by Shawnee, leaving two settlers dead. They returned in July, this time capturing three girls, including Daniel Boone's own daughter. Boone led a force to rescue the girls. On Christmas Day, Colonel John Todd, Mary Todd Lincoln's great-uncle, led an attack against the Mingo at Royal Springs. Four days later, the Mingo retaliated with an attack on McClelland's fort there. Several died on each side, and with the death of Chief Pluggy, the Mingo retreated.

As the War for American Independence began, the British tried to exert some degree of control over their Native American allies, offering larger rewards for live prisoners versus the reward for scalps, with varying degrees of success. A friendly visit by the peace-favoring Shawnee chief Blackfish ended in his murder, which enraged that tribe. A planned invasion into Kentucky was launched in 1778, and over one hundred braves and two Canadians marched on Boonesboro. Boone was captured (again) and persuaded them they did not have enough men to capture the fort. He escaped in June and warned the fort. The main force, now numbering over four hundred, returned in September and encamped around the fort at Boonesboro. An attempt at peace failed, and a nine-day battle ensued. The Shawnee tried several ways to win, including a fake retreat to draw out the settlers, tunneling under the walls and attempting to set fire to the fort walls. While this was going on, groups from the Indian forces attacked area cabins and settlements. The Indians finally gave up and retreated.

The year 1779 saw more attacks against travelers along both the Wilderness Road and Limestone Road. The Kentucky militia determined to counterattack, marching to a Shawnee village. Although they burned about forty cabins and stole 143 horses, they were forced to retreat. The attacking Shawnee chased them for about ten miles. Other attacks across the region continued throughout the year.

FIRST SETTLEMENTS

To say that frontiersmen poured into Kentucky would be an exaggeration. But in the late 1790s, establishment of stations (fortified villages), forts, and cabins accelerated. Fort Harrod was founded in 1774 by James Harrod and thirty-seven men. They returned to Virginia before winter but came back in June 1775 to start erecting the fort. Daniel Boone established Boonesboro that same year, and the Lee brothers started Leestown near the future site of Frankfort, although it would be another year before permanent improvements were made. However, all three settlements were south of the Kentucky River, and it was deemed advisable to establish a forward defensive site north of the river to forestall future Native American raids.

William McConnell and his brother, Francis, had explored the Elkhorn River watershed to the north. The Elkhorn has three branches, all flowing roughly east to west into the Kentucky River near Leestown. In 1775, McConnell and a small party were sent to cross the Kentucky River to scout for a likely site for another defensive settlement north of the river. They established a base camp on the north fork of the Elkhorn and began surveying. In June, they moved to the middle fork, built some rough cabins, and made other "improvements" as a basis for land claims. It is thought they camped around "the Boils," a spring that sprang or "boiled" out of the ground, and were discussing the area as a future town site when word came from Fort Harrod of the first engagement of the Revolutionary War at Lexington, Massachusetts. The group immediately decided to name the future town Lexington after that battle.

Indian raids delayed the project, however. Many retreated behind the walls of the forts and even back to Virginia. Perrin's *History of Fayette County* flatly states that in the "summer of 1776 no white man was found in all the length and breadth of present Fayette County. McConnell's cabin was deserted and falling to pieces." By the end of March 1779, prospects had improved and Colonel Levi Todd with the militia at Fort Harrod ordered Ensign Robert Patterson to take a company of twenty-five men, including at least two enslaved men, to build a blockhouse along the middle fork of the Elkhorn.

Patterson selected a site near the present corner of South Mill and West Main Streets, and there they erected the blockhouse. Later, the site would evolve into Lexington Station. At that time, a station was a collection of cabins facing one another with no windows on the rear walls and with log palisade walls connecting the cabins, forming a fortified area. Inside Lexington Station, a third row of cabins ran down the middle. The whole was erected around an ever-flowing spring for water. The spring ran into the middle fork of the Elkin River, which in time became known as Town Branch. Today it flows under Vine Street, under the convention center and

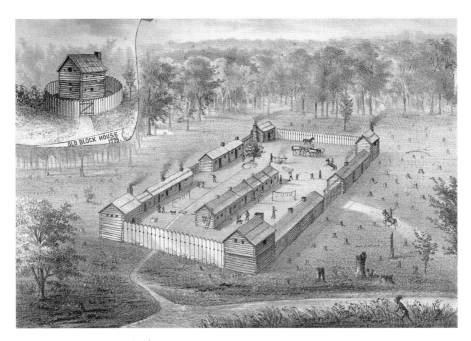

Lexington Station. *Perrin*, History of Fayette County, *1882*.

A plaque marking near Broadway and Vine Streets marks the site where Lexington's first blockhouse once stood. *Peter Brackney.*

around Rupp Arena and emerges from beneath the west parking lot to flow open through the Distillery District and on to the Kentucky River.

While the American Revolution east of the mountains generally receives the most attention, there was fighting in the west as well. The British in Canada rallied the Native American tribes to attack Kentucky. The most important fight, the Battle of Blue Licks, actually happened ten months after the surrender of General Cornwallis at Yorktown, which effectively ended the conflict in the east.

The series of events started when British captain William Caldwell with fifty soldiers and about three hundred Indians crossed the Ohio River into Kentucky with the intent of a surprise assault on Bryan's Station, just north of Lexington in present Fayette County. Advance word reached the station, however, and the settlers took shelter behind the station walls. Caldwell and his forces lay siege for two days, during which time the women of the station famously left the protection of the station to go get water in a successful effort to deceive the British into thinking they had not been discovered yet. Caldwell retreated after the second day, when he learned the Kentucky militia had been roused and was heading to engage his force.

Colonel John Todd arrived with forty-seven men on August 18, 1782, including second-in-command Lieutenant Colonel Daniel Boone. Boone urged waiting for reinforcements, only a day away, but the general feeling was not to allow the British and Indians any more lead and to pursue immediately. The next morning, the Kentuckians reached a salt lick called Lower Blue Licks near the Licking River. Again, Boone urged caution, but others mounted an attack into what was an ambush. Most of the Kentuckians, including Todd, were killed in the gunfire and hand-to-hand fighting. Boone lost his son but managed to stage a retreat with the surviving militia. It was the last victory for the British in the War of Independence.

The year before, in his capacity as state representative, Daniel Boone filed a bill to charter Lexington as a town, before he returned west. In 1782, the Virginia legislature, meeting in its new capital of Richmond, passed the bill introduced by Boone, and Lexington became a town in the same year its fortified station walls were completed.

In the following decade, Georgetown (1782), Danville (1783), Frankfort (1786), Paris (1786), Richmond (1789), Winchester (1792), Versailles (also 1792), and Nicholasville (1798) were founded as the threat of Indian raiding parties diminished.

After ten conventions over eight years, all held in Danville, including some intrigue involving secret paid agents of Spain who attempted to get Kentucky to leave the Union and join New Spain, the U.S. Congress, the Virginia legislature, and the Kentucky convention delegates reached agreement, and Kentucky became the fifteenth state on June 1, 1792.

The *Kentucky Gazette*, the first newspaper to be published west of the mountains, had started publication primarily as an advocate of statehood in 1787 and was flourishing. Lexington was poised on the brink of an almost half-century run as the leading educational, cultural, religious, civic, and commercial city of the new state.

ATHENS OF THE WEST

The act chartering Lexington set aside 640 acres of previously unappropriated land, which was added to 70 acres the town trustees had purchased to form the town boundary. The area was divided into both small and large lots, and each head of household and single men drew lots for one of each. The "In Lots" were clustered around a public square just north of Town Branch, and the "Out Lots" ringed around them. The intent was that an owner would build a dwelling on his In Lot, thus creating a town center, and use his Out Lot for crops, pasture, or other more agricultural uses. Colonel Patterson built a cabin in 1783 on an Out Lot on what would later be called Patterson Street. The area is now the parking lot for the Convention Center and Rupp Arena. After being moved a few times, the cabin is now located on the Transylvania University campus on Third Street and is the oldest surviving building in Lexington.

With the end of hostilities, Lexington began to be transformed from a frontier settlement to a small village. The walls of the station were taken down and streets laid out paralleling Town Branch and at right angles.

Unlike many other new towns where streets are aligned with the compass points, Lexington's streets vary by several degrees to line up with the Branch. Thus, when a north direction is given to a street, it really runs northeast.

The first schoolhouse in Kentucky was built on what is now Cheapside Park in 1783. The first courthouse was built in 1782 southwest of the corner of Main and Mill Streets. Within only five years, it was deemed inadequate and a new courthouse was erected on the town square. The former courthouse was sold to John Bradford, editor of the *Kentucky Gazette*, who moved his printing press there.

Virginia law at the time recognized the Church of England as an official religion and prohibited any other denomination from having a church in a town. Consequently, when Reverend Adam Rankin started a Presbyterian church, he located it just south of the city limits on Limestone Street. He built his house, however, in town on High (then called Hill) Street. It was relocated to South Mill Street in 1971. The Baptists were the second denomination to come to Lexington but, again, built their church outside of town in 1786 on today's Old Frankfort Pike. The Methodists arrived

Adam Rankin House. *Foster Ockerman Jr.*

next. Because Methodists were then a branch of the Church of England, the church was permitted in 1789 to occupy a town cabin for their church; it was located in the east end at what is today Short and Deweese Streets. As a result of this unique status, the Methodist Church was thus the first church actually in Lexington.

General James Wilkinson arrived in 1784 and opened the first permanent store. In 1785, James Bray opened the first tavern. The next year, John Higbee opened the first inn.

The year 1791 saw the construction of the first city market house: a two-story building with eight bays below for farmers and merchants to set up stalls and a second-floor room for a meeting hall. When Kentucky became a state, Lexington was the first and only provisional capital, and the first legislature met in that hall. The next year, Frankfort was chosen as the site for a permanent capitol building. Only four years later, the market had outgrown the building, and a new market house was built on today's Cheapside Park. Ironically, in modern times, the Lexington Farmer's Market would return from another site to Cheapside Park.

Tax records for 1795 reveal the extent of the rapid growth of Lexington. The three rows of cabins within the stockade had expanded into a small town with twenty-six stores and nine taverns plus inns and boardinghouses; hemp, baggage, and rope factories; a brewery and a distillery; brickyards; a nail plant; cabinet-makers; a variety of "smiths" (silversmiths, blacksmiths, and so on); dressmakers and tailors; a hatter, glover, and saddler; shoe and boot makers; weavers, and the first livery stable—and between three and four hundred houses.

The Virginia legislature had chartered the Transylvania Seminary as a public school in 1780. It opened its doors in Danville in 1785, but in 1793—upon attracting by the offer of a free Out Lot for a campus—it relocated to Lexington and erected a two-story building on "College Square," the present Gratz Park.

A young lawyer named Henry Clay arrived in Lexington in 1797 to begin his storied career as a lawyer, horse breeder, farmer, and, for a time, law professor at Transylvania University. In the first years of the 1800s, the Kentucky Insurance Company was formed, the first stagecoach line started operating out of Lexington into the region, brick sidewalks came to Lexington, and, in 1806, the third courthouse was built on the site of the second one.

Horse breeding and racing had a long tradition in Virginia, and it continued into central Kentucky. The first races were conducted along Main Street

The Bodley-Bullock House in Gratz Park. *Peter Brackney.*

in Lexington, but that practice was quickly banned by the town trustees. The first official racecourse ran from the top of the hill on South Broadway between High and Maxwell Streets a quarter mile down to the stream at the bottom of the hill. The first Jockey Club in Kentucky was formed in 1797. The first oval track, owned by the Williams brothers but run by the club, was laid out at the rear of what is now the Lexington Cemetery in 1795 and continued until about 1823, by which time it had closed. Races were held various places over the next three years until the Kentucky Association was formed in 1826. It constructed a new oval track on the northeast edge of Lexington, today's Fifth and Race Streets, where it conducted racing until 1932. The Keeneland Association was formed two years later and opened a new track on Versailles Road.

DISASTER, RECOVERY AND CIVIL WAR

By the 1830s, Louisville was growing faster than Lexington. The advent of the steam engine meant boats could travel upstream and well as down. Given

Louisville's proximity to the Falls of the Ohio, every ship going either way had to stop at Louisville and portage around the falls. Commercial traffic shifted from Lexington's land route to the Ohio River, bypassing central Kentucky. Then a cholera epidemic struck Lexington in 1833, killing a twelfth of its residents. Others fled the community or retreated to farms and resorts. There was so little activity in Lexington that grass grew in the main streets. Central Kentucky got a reputation as a bad place to live. Land prices started to fall. Then the national Panic of 1837 hit, caused by the bursting of financial speculation, and created a five-year depression. Of some 850 banks in the nation, almost half failed in whole or part.

By the 1840s, a recovery was underway. Several major buildings had been completed, including the Masonic Grand Lodge; new Methodist, Presbyterian, Episcopal, and Christian churches; the Lexington Theater; and the fifth Market House. The first telegraph line between Lexington and Louisville was strung in 1848, and the first railroad between those cities connected in 1852. The Maxwell Springs Company was formed and bought twenty-five acres, including a spring and pond, to create a city fairgrounds. The city would later give the land to the University of Kentucky as an inducement to keep it from moving to Louisville. The student center now sits on that land.

In 1852, Henry Clay died at age seventy-five. His remains were the first to lie in state in the U.S. Capitol. He was returned to Lexington for burial.

CIVIL WAR

Clay's death left few voices of compromise in the nation, state, or Lexington. Individuals began to favor one side or the other, although election results suggest central Kentucky as a whole favored the continuation of both the Union and slavery. The raid on Harpers Ferry in the fall of 1859 started to change views, as fear of slave revolts fermented by northern abolitionists raised public safety concerns. The result in Lexington was the formation or enlargement of volunteer militia companies led by prominent men. Georgetown, Paris, Winchester, and Versailles, among other towns, formed their own militias. The Kentucky State Guard was created to organize local units, not for the purpose of supporting one side or the other as states began to secede, but to protect people and property.

On May 6, 1861, Governor Beriah Magoffin called a special session of the legislature to address secession. The General Assembly refused to call a secession convention and instead adopted a formal position and statement of neutrality on May 16. However well intended, it was an impossible position to sustain.

While the legislature was in session, on President Lincoln's authority, five thousand muskets were secretly smuggled from Cincinnati across the Ohio River to Covington. From there, they were loaded on freight cars to be delivered to Bourbon, Fayette, Clark, and Montgomery Counties in central Kentucky in violation of state law. After the firing on the federal Fort Sumter by Confederate forces, Lincoln issued a call for troops. Kentucky refused to send support to either side.

Lexington, and by extension central Kentucky, sat at the junction of the three major western railroad lines running south from Louisville, Cincinnati, and Huntington and in turn running at the only major supply routes south. The area was also a rich agricultural region able to supply and support armies with food, horses and mules, and other materiel. With Confederate forces blocking the Mississippi River, central Kentucky was seen as the major land route in the West. As Lincoln said, "I hope to have God on my side, but I must have Kentucky." Each side, in fact, needed Kentucky—the Union for supplies and a path for invading, the South to obtain those same resources and to establish a defensible border at the Ohio River. Neutrality was never a realistic option.

The war came soon to Lexington. Union troops first occupied the city on August 21, 1861, with about 200 troops arriving and setting up camp at the city fairgrounds at Maxwell Springs. A month later, 1,500 more troops joined them. By July 1862, more than 3,000 Union troops occupied a city with an 1860 census population of just over 9,000 people, including White residents and both a free Black population and those who were enslaved. Two months later, CSA general Kirby Smith won the Battle of Richmond and invaded Lexington with his roughly 4,000 troops, mounted and foot, driving the Union forces north.

Smith and his officers stayed in the Phoenix Hotel, and that September, the regularly scheduled fall Thoroughbred racing meet was held at the Kentucky Association track on the eastern edge of town. It was the only time Thoroughbred racing was held under the Confederate flag, and Lexington's was the only Southern track to continue racing throughout the war.

People drew in their Union flags and hung Confederate flags at their windows. By early October, however, Union forces returned and drove Smith and his army out of central Kentucky. People changed their colors once again.

Men left central Kentucky to join each side, some families being divided in loyalties; few families escaped losing a loved one to the conflict.

DEVELOPMENTS IN EDUCATION

Transylvania Seminary was chartered in 1780 and opened in a log cabin in Boyle County. By 1789, it had relocated to Lexington on the offer of a city block for a campus. Bacon College, spun off from Georgetown College, was chartered in 1837, operating off and on until relocating from Harrodsburg in 1858 and taking the name Kentucky University. In 1863, Congress passed the Morrill Act granting federal lands to the states for purposes of creating, expanding, and supporting agricultural and mechanical colleges. Kentucky took the opportunity to merge Transylvania and Kentucky Universities under the latter's name and acquire over four hundred acres of the Henry Clay estate for a "rural" campus for the A&M College. Transylvania/KU also began a department of religious studies.

Seemingly it was a good deal for all, but tensions existed between the old Transylvania colleges, which were governed by a religious denomination, and the legislature-governed A&M College. In 1878, the two divided. Old Transylvania retained the name Kentucky University and retreated to its

Memorial Hall was completed in 1929 and is the most iconic building on the campus of the University of Kentucky. *Peter Brackney.*

downtown campus. It also established its religious studies department as the College of the Bible.

Kentucky A&M now needed a source of revenue and offered to locate in whichever city made the best bid. Covington and Louisville entered bids, raising the prospect that the only state-supported institution of higher education would leave central Kentucky. The future of basketball could have been changed forever. However, Lexington was unwilling to allow that to happen and offered its city fairgrounds for a new campus. Lexington and Fayette County also offered $50,000 in government bond financing for constructing buildings. The A&M College accepted that offer.

In time, Transylvania readopted its old name, the College of the Bible separated and changed its name to Lexington Theological Seminary, and the A&M College became the University of Kentucky.

FAST HORSES, BEAUTIFUL WOMEN, AND GOOD BOURBON—ALL UNDER ATTACK

The waves of progressive reform that swept across the country in the late nineteenth and early twentieth centuries did not bypass Lexington. Several significant changes were happening to the general fabric of central Kentucky.

Hemp had long been the major crop in the region, spurred by the demand for the U.S. Navy and the sailing industry for hemp fiber ropes. As sails gave way to steam engines on the waters, the growing demand for tobacco products led to a shift to the latter crop. Kentucky as a whole produced 105 million pounds of tobacco in 1870. By 1916, production had grown to over 462 million pounds.

Likewise, Kentucky led in the production of distilled spirits. In 1891, there were 172 distilleries in Kentucky, many of those in central Kentucky, producing 34 percent of the nation's bourbon and other spirits. By 1915, the state was producing a whopping 70 percent.

But the progressive movement was targeting the sale of liquor in the hope that society would improve if drunkenness was reduced. Serious agitation began in Kentucky around 1890, and by 1914, all but 14 of Kentucky's 120 counties had voted to go dry. Lexington, however, defeated that referendum by a two-to-one margin in 1914, leaving the city an oasis in the midst of dry counties. There were over 150 saloons in a town of barely 35,000 people.

The passage of Prohibition in 1920 put a stop to the sale of liquor nationwide. Many of Lexington's saloons became sandwich shops with a back room for selling liquor illegally.

In 1881, the Kentucky Woman Suffrage Association, later renamed the Kentucky Equal Rights Association, was started. Central Kentucky women were among the leaders of the national movement for voting rights for women, including Laura Clay (daughter of abolitionist Cassius Clay) and Madeline McDowell Breckinridge (great-granddaughter of Henry Clay). Women's suffrage would be achieved on a national scale with the passage of the Nineteenth Amendment in 1920.

On the other side of women's issues, however, were the houses of prostitution in Lexington, including that of nationally known madam Belle Brezing. While it was nominally unlawful, Lexington tolerated the practice and had gradually concentrated the houses into a red-light district on the east end of town.

The chamber of commerce, founded in 1881, had long advocated for creation of a military training camp in Lexington. With the advent of World War I, the army established such a camp on a 220-acre farm on Versailles Road west of the city. It housed over 2,500 soldiers in 300 wood barracks. General Roger D. Williams, the commanding officer, declared the red-light district off-limits to his men and pressured the city government to shut the houses, which was done.

The chamber also led the way in calling for the county to acquire the private turnpike companies, which owned and controlled all major roads leading to and from Lexington, and free travel from the tolls. Its reason was transparent: tolls added to the cost of moving goods and livestock, which was bad for business. In 1890, Fayette County acquired its first road and, over the next decade, purchased eleven major roads at the cost of between $1,500 and $2,000 per mile.

The progressives also targeted pari-mutuel wagering. In 1897, there were over three hundred working racetracks in the United States, but gradually and state-by-state, laws were passed outlawing wagering, leading to the closure of tracks. By 1910, there were only twenty-three tracks in the country, and two of those were in Lexington. In 1923, a bill was introduced in the Kentucky General Assembly to outlaw wagering in the state. It failed to become law by only one vote.

Thus, in a relatively short period of time, the association of central Kentucky with fast horses, beautiful women, and good bourbon had been attacked. If the bourbon industry and the horse industry had disappeared from central Kentucky, its image and success would have been very different. But racing and wagering continued in Kentucky, and Prohibition was repealed in 1933. The Great Depression contributed to the demise of the

Kentucky Association Thoroughbred racetrack at the edge of downtown Lexington in 1934, but the new Keeneland Association Racetrack opened in 1936. The first Junior League Horse Show was held in 1937.

Although little noticed at the time, one final major event in 1930 occurred in the hiring by the University of Kentucky of a twenty-nine-year-old high school basketball coach from Illinois named Adolph Rupp as its new men's basketball head coach. The prescient athletic director was Stanley Boles.

When World War II began, Lexington had about ten thousand citizens. The city and county had jointly purchased over five hundred acres on Versailles Road for a new airfield, which was briefly used by the U.S. Army as a military facility before commercial flights began after the war. The end of the war also saw record numbers of new students enter University of Kentucky and Transylvania College. UK alone increased from about three thousand students in 1944 to over ten thousand by the end of the decade.

MAJOR MUNICIPAL GROWTH

The 1950s opened a period of rapid growth for Lexington and central Kentucky. The Lexington Industrial Foundation bought 159 acres on the north end of town for a new business park and, significantly, determined not to seek "smokestack" industries but only clean businesses. Anticipating the approaching interstate highway system, which would connect at Lexington, major businesses like Square D, Dixie Cup, R.J. Reynolds Tobacco, and others opened new facilities. IBM selected Lexington for its new electric typewriter manufacturing plant, bringing cutting-edge technology to the area. In 1958, Lexington adopted the first-in-the-nation Urban Service Boundary, setting a boundary beyond which no commercial development could occur. Acres of significant horse farms were preserved as a result. In 1958, *US News & World Report* identified Lexington as one of the fourteen fastest-growing cities in the nation.

In the mid-1960s, the next major change happened. Lexington bought the downtown rights of way from the railroad companies and removed the tracks from downtown. The tracks lay along what is today the Vine Street corridor. Urban renewal projects followed, and the face of central Lexington was changed as warehouses were demolished and modern office buildings constructed. In 1974, plans were announced for a new civic center complex with a new hotel and Rupp Arena. By 1970, Lexington had over 108,000 residents, and the effects of growth had to be addressed. The solution,

Downtown railroad tracks. *C&O Railroad Historical Society.*

Vine Street corridor after tracks were removed and redeveloped. *Foster Ockerman Jr.*

new to Kentucky and rare in the nation, was to merge the city and county governments into an urban county government in 1974. By 1980, the population was almost 205,000, a 259 percent increase in just forty years.

For the balance of the century, the major community debate was growth versus no growth. Finally, in 2000, a Rural Land Management Plan was adopted to guide growth and another first-ever-in-the-nation local Purchase of Development Rights Program bought development rights from rural farms, permanently prohibiting any more intense land use than agricultural on the affected tracts.

The first two decades of the twenty-first century brought a rebalancing of land use downtown as the effect of "grow up not out" policies dictated more intense development in the city core. Underutilized blocks of two-to-four-story buildings and surface parking lots gave way to more parking garages and taller office buildings and new hotels. In 2019, a reconstruction and expansion of the Civic Center was begun; it would result in over 100,000 square feet of exhibit and meeting space and a reworking of Rupp Arena. Both universities started major construction projects, hospitals and shopping malls expanded, and, within the limits of the Urban Service Boundary, Lexington continued to grow.

2

LEXINGTON AND FAYETTE COUNTY

Lexington and Fayette County are a merged urban county government, one of a handful in the United States. Almost all governmental functions are under the one urban county government. A distinctive feature of Lexington is its Urban Service Boundary. Established in the 1950s, its purpose is to draw a line around the city beyond which development cannot occur. While the exact boundary is adjusted every few years, this border, combined with an aggressive purchase of development rights from surrounding farms, has served to preserve neighboring horse farms and the distinct central Kentucky landscape.

McCONNELL SPRINGS

In 1775, William McConnell, his brother, and a band of kinsmen and other men from Fort Harrod were exploring this area and made camp at a spring near the middle fork of the Elkhorn River. Their intent was to stake claims to land. Under Virginia law (and what would become Kentucky was still part of Virginia at this time), to claim land you had to survey it, marking trees as boundary marks, build some rudimentary improvement (often a low log cabin), and plant a crop. Corn was typically used because it was not native to the area, thus evidencing a man-made effort, and it grew taller than native vegetation. The story is the men were around their campfire one night considering how the valley would be a good site for a town and speculating on possible names, generally after English noblemen, when word came from

Fort Harrod that the Battle of Lexington in Massachusetts had happened, initiating the fight for independence, a popular sentiment in the western lands. Immediately, the men determined the future town should be named "Lexington" after the battle.

The McConnell Springs area is now a city park with an educational building and two miles of trails. Over the years, it had become an industrial dumping area. In 1994, a group of citizens raised the funds and got the community support to clean and restore the area. It has three natural springs where water comes to the surface from the limestone strata below. In this case, McConnell Springs is the only known place in the area where water surfaces, flows across the land, goes back underground, and then resurfaces a distance away. There is also a burr oak tree estimated to be at least 250 years old, meaning it was possibly a sapling when the McConnell team arrived. The park is listed in the National Register of Historic Places and located off Manchester Street past the Distillery District.

BOONE STATION

In December 1779, Daniel Boone and members of his family established Boone Station in eastern Fayette County. It is a long story, but the militia at Fort Harrod had conceived that Colonel Boone might have made a side deal with the Indians to the possible detriment of the fort and brought him up on court-martial charges. Boone was found innocent, but he was no longer comfortable residing in the fort.

A station in pioneer Kentucky was a fortified settlement, more than an open camp but less that a military fort. As described elsewhere in discussing Bryan's Station and Lexington Station, a station was frequently a collection of cabins facing inward with no rear windows. The cabins were then connected by log walls to create an enclosure. Never intended as a defensible construct, the purpose was to provide temporary protection in the event of Indian attack while a rider went to the nearest fort for the militia.

Boone Station was located next to a natural spring on what is now a forty-six-acre tract near the rural community of Athens (pronounced *Eh-thenz*). In its case, instead of full cabins, the group erected a camp of half-faced shelters connected by a rough log fence. In the spring of 1780, these were largely replaced with full cabins and a stockade fence. At most, the station housed some fifteen families. By 1781, however, it appeared Boone's claim to the land was worthless, and he lost ownership. Boone and his immediate family ultimately moved to Missouri; others remained in the area for a while. By 1791, Boone Station no longer existed.

For a period of time, the station was a Kentucky State Park, but it returned to private hands in 2019. It is located at 240 Gentry Road, a narrow rural lane. There is a marker at the site, a monument can be seen from the road, and there are several graves of the pioneers there.

BRYAN'S STATION

Bryan's Station was another fortified settlement located on the north fork of the Elkhorn River in northern Fayette County near the present Briar Hill Road. It was established by the four Bryan brothers and the settlers who came with them from North Carolina around 1775 or 1776. There were about forty cabins connected by log walls located near a spring, which was their source of fresh water. During the Revolutionary War in 1782, a force of some four or five hundred Native Americans and British rangers under British command secretly, they believed, surrounded the station. However, their presence was known to the settlers, and a rider had been sent for reinforcements. To deceive the attackers into believing they had not been detected, the women and girls of the station were sent on their customary morning trek to the spring for water to show the ordinary routine was not disturbed. The ruse worked, and when word of the coming militia force reached the attackers, they retreated. The militia pursued but were ultimately defeated at the Battle of Blue Licks, three days and sixty miles later.

A stone monument to the women and girls for their bravery has been erected at the site, which is on a private farm.

PATTERSON CABIN

The oldest surviving pioneer cabin is that built by Colonel Robert Patterson before 1780. Patterson had been sent with a party of men from Fort Harrod to build the first blockhouse at Lexington, which became the corner cabin of future Lexington Station. Patterson not only helped found Lexington but was also involved in starting the Ohio communities of Cincinnati and Dayton. He served on the town board of trustees and helped charter Transylvania University. He also served as the state representative from Fayette County for eight years following statehood in 1792.

The cabin itself has had a nomadic existence. Built first on Patterson's approximately four-hundred-acre farm south of Lexington in what became known as Davis Bottom, west of South Broadway along the path of Oliver Lewis Way, it was moved to his son's farm in Ohio in 1901. Over time, it has been a home, a slave quarters, a toolshed, and general storage. It may even have been a school for enslaved children. It was returned to Lexington in 1939 at the request of the Commonwealth and the Daughters of the American Revolution and now stands on the Transylvania University campus near North Broadway and West Third Streets.

ADAM RANKIN HOUSE

The Adam Rankin House is the oldest surviving house, as distinct from pioneer cabins like the Patterson Cabin, in Lexington. The original structure was built of logs in 1784 on the north side of High Street between Mill and Upper Streets, mid-block roughly facing the present First United Methodist Church. It is two stories high, and there was a frame addition made in 1794. Rankin was the founder and first minister of the First Presbyterian Church, the oldest congregation in Lexington in continuous service. It was owned in the 1830s by Samuel D. McCullough, a noted astronomer, author, and mathematician. He conducted an academy in the house and later manufactured the world-famous Burrowes' Lexington Mustard on the property.

By the 1970s, the structure was in disrepair and in the path of urban renewal. To save the building, the Blue Grass Trust for Historic Preservation bought the house and moved it to its current location at 317 South Mill Street in the South Hill Historic District. The trust sold the property at auction in 1972 with deed restrictions to prevent its destruction or exterior alteration.

In 2020, the Lexington History Museum announced that it had acquired the Rankin House and that the first floor would become the fifth house museum in Lexington, with exhibits on its history.

HISTORIC FAYETTE COUNTY COURTHOUSE

The Historic Courthouse, located on Main Street, is the fourth courthouse to occupy this site on the town square. The prior courthouse, a wood frame

The circa 1898 courthouse during a Fourth of July parade. *Peter Brackney.*

building, burned down in 1897, and this building of limestone blocks and brick was intended to avoid that fate. Constructed between 1898 and 1900, it is of Romanesque design. Originally, it housed the courts as well as the county government and county offices. As the courts grew with Lexington, and following the merger, the county offices were largely taken over by the court and related functions, eventually even causing the county clerk to relocate. With the new century, new courthouses were built along North Limestone, and the urban county retook control of the old courthouse. For a time, the Lexington History Museum operated out of the building, but in 2012, environmental hazards in the building forced its closure. By 2019, following a significant and detailed restoration, the Historic Courthouse reopened with restaurants, offices, a function space on the top floor and the visitor's center. The massive and ornamental interior dome was restored and provides a grand setting for events.

CHEAPSIDE PARK (FIFTH THIRD BANK PAVILION)

Cheapside Park with its Fifth Third Pavilion is located adjacent to and west of the Historic Courthouse. From the city's beginnings, it has served as a community gathering place and, intermittently, as its marketplace. The VisitLEX website gives this description:

> The public square at the center of downtown was platted in 1780 as the site of the courthouse for the newly established town of Lexington. The square has always been, and still is, a place where significant events and community activities have occurred. Archive records tell of a fight between a school teacher and a wildcat, controversial slave auctions, military drills, Civil War skirmishes, riots, hangings, speeches and fires that destroyed previous courthouses. This history has been inclusive of African Americans both enslaved and free.
>
> By 1789, an area of the square had been designated as a marketplace and named after the market in London, England—Cheapside (old English ceapan means to buy). William Tucker (1787–1837), a free African

Cheapside Park. *Foster Ockerman Jr.*

American, was one of the merchants who advertised the sale of household items and spices from his stall. Farmers and others, during their monthly visits to transact legal business, bought, sold and swapped livestock and agricultural products. The sale activity, known as Court Day, ended in 1921. Historian J. Winston Coleman, Jr. documented two dozen dealers in Lexington who bought and sold the enslaved between 1833 and 1865.

The origin of the name is deep in English history. "Cheapside" was a multiblock market area in London, and Lexington's founders borrowed the name for their marketplace. While the first markethouse was on the south side of Main at Mill, the second and third market buildings were on the park. In the late 1800s, a new markethouse was built along then Water Street near the railroad. With advent of modern groceries and markets, it was no longer needed and eventually torn down. In 2009, however, Lexington's Farmer's Market returned to Cheapside, and in season, the pavilion and surrounding area are filled with farmers' stalls.

Cheapside's history is part of Lexington's darkest chapter as well, for it was here at the market where people were sold as property.

MELODEON HALL

Melodeon Hall is a cast iron–façade building on the southwest corner of Upper and Main Streets opposite the Old Courthouse. It is actually two buildings erected about 1849, but a common front was added sometime

Melodeon Hall. *Foster Ockerman Jr.*

after 1857. The original configuration of the building included a two-story performance hall on the second floor with a theater seating three hundred attendees. Abraham Lincoln and his wife, Mary, attended a theater performance there during one of their visits. In one of history's ironies, John Wilkes Booth performed there as well, though at a different time.

In the late nineteenth century, a business college occupied the building. A century later, the large second floor was divided horizontally with the addition of a third floor and converted to offices.

While there were other downtown buildings with cast-iron façades, Melodeon Hall is the only one that survives.

FAYETTE NATIONAL BANK BUILDING (21C HOTEL)

The building that now houses the 21C Hotel was originally built in 1913 as the headquarters for the Fayette National Bank. The bank was chartered in 1870 and raised an ornate three-story building on the corner. The first commercial building in Lexington with a stone façade and mansard roof, it was designed by famed local architect John McMurty. When that building no longer served the bank's purposes, it was razed and the current building erected. The Fayette National Bank building was Lexington's first skyscraper, made possible by the invention of commercial-grade elevators. At the bank's grand opening, the public was allowed to ride the elevators to

Fayette Bank Building. *Foster Ockerman Jr.*

the roof for a panoramic view of the city. It remained the tallest building in Lexington for almost sixty years, until the First Security Plaza, now the Chase Bank building, was erected in 1972 by a successor institution to the Fayette National Bank.

CARNEGIE LIBRARY BUILDING

Lexington's public library was started by subscription in 1795 and is possibly the oldest such library west of the Allegheny Mountains. In 1898, a change in state law enabled Lexington to convert to a free public library. In 1906, the Andrew Carnegie Foundation, established by steel magnate Andrew Carnegie, gifted the city $60,000 for the purpose of building a new library. The grant required the city to provide the land and funds for operating the library when built. Gratz Park on Second Street was chosen for the new Bedford limestone building. The main library moved to its quarters on Main Street next to Phoenix Park in the 1980s. The Carnegie Building now houses the Carnegie Center for Literacy and Learning.

Carnegie Center. *Foster Ockerman Jr.*

LEXINGTON OPERA HOUSE

Theater played an important role in the cultural life of Lexington almost from the start. Over the years, several opera houses and theaters have burned or otherwise been destroyed. The Lexington Opera House on North Broadway was built in 1886 to replace an earlier theater leveled by fire. It opened with a production of *Our Angel* on August 19, 1887. It originally had seating for 1,250 patrons and included two balconies and eight boxes ranked on either side of the stage. Later renovations have reduced to number of seats to around 1,000.

The interior was decorated in Turkish morocco. An 1893 newspaper articles described it as one of the "costliest, handsomest and most convenient Thespian temples in the South." Performers, in particular, praised its excellent acoustics.

In 1890, a production of *Henley Regatta* required the flooding of the stage. In 1893, almost one hundred animals and a mile-long parade were employed for *A Country Circus*. The audience for the 1904 production of *Ben Hur* witnessed an on-stage chariot race! John Philip Sousa, Will Rogers, Mae West, and the Marx Brothers all performed in the Opera House.

After 1926, the building began a long period of use as a movie theater and even longer period of deterioration. By the 1970s, it was scheduled to be demolished for a parking lot; however, that period saw the emergence of the historic preservation movement in Lexington, and the building was saved. Great care was taken to make molds of the ornamental plaster elements to replicate the ornate original elements. A collection of historic photographs provided detail for woodwork and other elements, and the entire facility was accurately restored down to the stage curtains.

Today, thanks to a trust fund established as part of the fundraising for the restoration, even local nonprofit theater groups can have a large portion of the cost of mounting a show underwritten. Traveling shows from New York stages regularly perform here.

PHOENIX PARK

The historic importance of Phoenix Park lies in the buildings that preceded the current park use.

The southeast corner of Main Street and Limestone Street was by 1800 the home of Postlethwaite's Tavern, which had sleeping rooms on the second floor. It was a popular gathering place for the leading citizens of Lexington and frequently the place for organizational meetings of new organizations and ventures. Between 1800 and 1820, there were changes in the hotel's ownership and name. In 1806, it was Wilson's Tavern when former vice president Aaron Burr stayed here while traveling the western United States either raising funds and men for a new western settlement or raising a revolutionary force to lead Kentucky and Tennessee to secede from the Union, depending on whose story is to be believed. Burr was charged with treason by Kentucky's U.S. attorney and successfully defended by Henry Clay.

The Phoenix Hotel, version one, opened on the site in the 1820s. Its name derived from the fact that, after at least one destructive fire, the hotel was rebuilt and returned to business. Over the years, the hotel would be enlarged, torn down and rebuilt, and enlarged again.

In 1915, it was the site for meetings of the Kentucky Equal Rights Association. Over the years, many groups, fraternities, social organizations, and civic organizations made the hotel their regular meeting place and site for conventions. High schools held their proms in the hotel's ballroom, and politicians held election rallies there as well. The Phoenix and the Lafayette were Lexington's grand hotels (the Lafayette Hotel, at the corner of Main Street and Martin Luther King Boulevard, now being the present location of city hall).

The Phoenix was also a focal point for members of the equine industry who stayed there during visits to Lexington for race meets. So prominent a role did it play that a number of races and titles were named for it. The Phoenix Hotel Stakes, first run in Lexington in 1831, is considered to be the oldest Thoroughbred race for three-year-olds in the country.

The hotel closed in 1977. In 1987, it was demolished by businessman and future governor Wallace Wilkinson, who intended to build a large office tower on the land. When that did not come about, the city and the state each purchased parcels of the land where the hotel and other buildings had been. A state-owned parking garage now occupies a rear portion of the area, and there are apartments above the garage. The Lexington Public Library acquired the parcel between the garage and Main Street and erected a new, modern building. The city retained the limestone frontage for the present Phoenix Park.

TOWN BRANCH AND TOWN BRANCH PARK

Lexington was founded along the waters of the Town Branch, the middle fork of the Elkhorn River. It begins at a spring that bubbles up near present Walton Avenue and Third Street and flows first in a southerly direction and then turns and flows west to the Kentucky River near Frankfort. The first plat of Lexington, which laid out the lots and streets, left a commons area along the banks of the Branch, and early on, the town trustees hired workers to straighten the course of the creek, to line its banks with limestone rock, and to build bridges over the waterway. It was never a navigable stream, however, except during flood periods, and consequently became less and less of a valuable feature as the town grew. By the end of the Civil War, several bridges crossed over it, businesses even spanned the creek from bank to bank, and the coming railroads lined the branch with rails. Eventually, the number of railroad tracks desired exceeded the land available, and the creek was entirely enclosed from its origin to west of the Rupp Arena parking lot.

The Town Branch of the Elkhorn River, looking west (downstream) from just beyond the Rupp Arena/Civic Center parking lot. *Foster Ockerman Jr.*

In recent years, plans have been developed to bring Town Branch back to the surface, figuratively in part and in reality in a new park. The corridor along Vine Street will link bicycle routes, including the Town Branch Trail and the Legacy Trail, as part of a cycling loop around downtown, while the park to the east of an enlarged convention center is intended to provide a large green space near the heart of downtown Lexington.

MARY TODD LINCOLN HOUSE

The Mary Todd Lincoln house on West Main Street is located just west of the convention center and Rupp Arena. It was originally built as a tavern around 1803 at the very western edge of the platted town of Lexington. By 1832, the business on the property failed, and it was foreclosed on by the Bank of the United States. The bank's lead attorney was Henry Clay. Robert Todd bought the property at the court-ordered auction and added to it two more lots to configure a nice town residence and garden running

Mary Todd Lincoln House. *Foster Ockerman Jr.*

back to the waters of Town Branch. Mary Todd was thirteen or fourteen when her family moved from their prior residence two blocks to the north and lived in this house until she left to live in Springfield, Illinois, with her sister. It was in Springfield, of course, where she met her future husband, Abraham Lincoln.

The Todd property in his day also contained a separate slave quarters, an outdoor kitchen (a usual practice to prevent kitchen fires from emblazing the residence), a wash house, a smokehouse, and stables, including a carriage house. The property bordered a narrow side street running from Main Street back to the Branch, so the stables likely led into that street. The residence itself contains fourteen rooms, and there is a partially restored garden in the back.

Robert Todd survived the 1833 cholera epidemic in Lexington but succumbed when cholera returned in 1849, ten years after Mary had moved to Springfield.

After his death, legal disputes in the Todd family resulted in the house being sold at public auction, and the property was put to many uses over the ensuing decades, including a boardinghouse, grocery store, an inn or tavern, and even a brothel. Finally, it was suited only for storage. The rear of the property has become part of the parking and staging area for the convention center. In 1977, Beula C. Nunn, the wife of Governor Louie Nunn, led a movement to acquire the property, restore it, and open it to the public as the first house museum in the United States to honor a first lady. Over the years, family portraits and furnishings have been secured from the Todd and Lincoln families for the house.

HOPEMONT, THE HUNT-MORGAN HOUSE

John Wesley Hunt, known as the first millionaire west of the Allegheny Mountains, built this house on North Mill Street at Second Street in 1814. It is a Federal-style house with many fine architectural features, including a Palladian window over the entrance. Hunt was involved in many businesses and interests, including growing hemp, which, in the early 1800s, was a major crop in central Kentucky. The property also features a beautiful garden and a restored carriage house.

Hunt's great-grandson was Dr. Thomas Hunt Morgan, a geneticist and one of the few Kentuckians to be awarded a Nobel Prize. A community desire to save the house, after the demolition of the Thomas Hart House across Second Street for a parking lot, led to the establishment of today's Blue Grass Trust for Historic Preservation. The trust bought Hopemont and restored the building and grounds to its circa 1814 appearance.

Open for tours, Hopemont is also home to the Alexander T. Hunt Civil War Museum and a new Kentucky Hemp Museum.

WAVELAND STATE HISTORIC SITE

Waveland, also known as the Joseph Bryan House, is a Greek Revival–style home on the former Bryan family plantation in Fayette County.

The Bryans and Daniel Boone and his family are intertwined in the founding of Kentucky. The two families became acquainted when the Boones moved next to the Bryans in North Carolina. It is reported that Bryan was the financial support behind several of Boone's expeditions into what would become Kentucky. William Bryan married Daniel Boone's sister, Mary. Their son, Daniel Boone Bryan, became a famous historian, frontiersman, and poet. He received the approximately two thousand acres south of Lexington.

Today, Waveland contains the mansion, an icehouse, an unusual two-story slave quarters, a barn, and a smokehouse on ten acres. In 1957, it was established as a museum interpreting Kentucky life in the early nineteenth century.

POPE VILLA

In 1810, noted architect Benjamin Henry Latrobe designed a villa for Senator John Pope to be built just outside the young town of Lexington. Today, the villa survives in a dense residential neighborhood near the University of Kentucky campus on Grosvenor Avenue.

Latrobe was born and educated in England and came to the United States in 1795. He became one of the country's first professional architects. President Thomas Jefferson selected Latrobe to design and supervise construction of the White House and the national Capitol. He and Pope met when the latter was in Washington serving in the Senate from 1807 to 1813. Pope and his Senate colleague Henry Clay collaborated to develop a proposal for extensive internal improvements in the West, including highways, bridges, and canals.

Pope Villa is described as the best surviving example of Latrobe's residential designs. While the unique building is a cube on the outside,

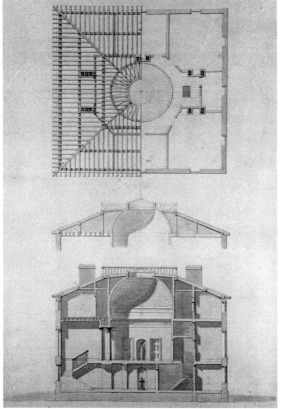

Above: Pope Villa *Foster Ockerman Jr.*

Left: Pope Villa floor plans. *Blue Grass Trust.*

the interior contains "a surprising sequence of rectilinear and curvilinear rooms" with a domed, circular rotunda in the center of the second floor.

Years of existence as student rental housing resulted in alternations that had to be removed. The building and grounds are owned by the Blue Grass Trust for Historic Preservation, which is conducting the ongoing restoration of the villa.

ASHLAND, THE HENRY CLAY ESTATE

In 1799, Henry Clay arrived in Lexington from Virginia to practice law. Within five years, Clay began acquiring farmland on the east side of the town and, by 1809, had constructed a house that would serve in time as the center section of his house. Clay met the architect Benjamin Latrobe in Washington and had him design two wings to added to the house. Each end block was connected to the main house by one-story hyphens. The estate would eventually contain more than six hundred acres between the Richmond and Tates Creek Roads, with many barns and outbuildings and a Thoroughbred training track. Clay was as much a breeder of cattle, mules, and horses as he was a politician and lawyer.

Upon Clay's death in 1852, his widow moved in with one of their sons, John Clay, and Ashland was sold to another son, James. James Clay found his father's mansion in an extreme state of disrepair, to the extent that he had the building disassembled, saving as much of the original material as possible, and rebuilt following the original plans. Although he incorporated certain Italianate, Greek Revival, and Victorian details, the house today is essentially the re-creation of Henry Clay's home.

John Clay, however, was a strong follower of the Confederacy and fled Lexington in 1862, never to return. In 1866, the new Kentucky Agricultural and Mechanical College (then a part of Transylvania University, later to become the University of Kentucky) purchased Ashland for its rural campus. Its first president, John Bowman, lived on the second floor, and the first floor was used as classrooms and a museum.

By 1878, Kentucky A&M was financially weak and started looking for a new campus and new funding. Lexington agreed to donate its former fairgrounds as a campus, and the city and county combined with new funding for buildings and the college moved to its current site. It rented Ashland until 1882, when Henry Clay McDowell and his wife, Anne Clay, a granddaughter of Henry Clay, bought the land and returned it to family ownership.

Ashland, Henry Clay Estate. *Foster Ockerman Jr.*

After their deaths, it passed to their oldest child, Nannette Bullock, and her husband. The Bullocks and their son were the last residents of the mansion. Through her efforts, the Henry Clay Memorial Foundation was created to preserve the house and the remaining seventeen acres. On April 12, 1950, Vice President Alben Barkley led a large crowd in dedicating Ashland as a historic house museum.

3

THE SPORT OF KINGS
AND OTHER SPORTS

Horse racing has been a part of Lexington from its earliest days. The town was hardly chartered before there was horse racing down Main Street. In 1793, the town trustees labeled it a "growing evil" and a "pernicious practice" when they banned racing from the town streets. Racing moved to the town commons along Town Branch and then to roads outside of the city limits. At the time, the lots facing High Street comprised the southern end of town, so racing moved to the top of the hill outside of town between today's High and Maxwell Streets, and racing ran down the hill to the spring at the bottom. At the time, races were straight sprints, as the land required for a full racetrack oval was expensive and had to be cleared. In 1787, the Lexington Jockey Club was founded to conduct racing on an organized basis.

Sometime during the 1770s or early 1780s, Colonel John Todd conducted racing, likely another straight race path, on his property along the road to Georgetown, just west of Lexington—likely between today's Short and Third Streets. Todd was the great-uncle of Mary Todd, who married Abraham Lincoln. Unfortunately, Colonel Todd died in the Battle of Blue Licks in 1783. A widower, he left a young daughter as his only living heir, and interest in racing there ended. As Lexington grew toward Todd lands and it was subdivided and sold as house lots, the deeds frequently referred to the greater property as the "Old Race Field."

The Lexington Jockey Club now wanted to build an oval tract, as the mile-long heat races testing endurance were becoming more popular that the quarter-mile sprints focusing on speed. It constructed, or caused to be constructed, an oval track on a large and fairly flat piece of land farther west from Todd on the other side of the Georgetown Pike in what is now the rear of the Lexington Cemetery and extending north into what is today a small residential neighborhood and was conducting races as early as 1795. This course was a one-mile oval and went by several names: the Williams (or Williams Brothers) Course, Boswells' Woods, and Lee's Woods. When the Jockey Club conducted its contests, it referred to them as being run on the "Lexington Course," which may have been a designation of the race course itself as distinct from the total property. An advertisement announcing a forthcoming race in October 1795 noted, among other information, that horses were to be entered by the day before the race or pay a double fee to enter on race day. Local historian William Ambrose reports that the Jockey Club ceased conducting race meets by 1823.

In the early 1810s, there were races at the "Pond Course," listed in one advertisement as being two miles from Lexington, but the compass direction is not given. One writer speculates it may have been on a farm two to three miles northeast of Lexington on the Maysville Road, now Paris Pike, known locally at the time as Wrights Pond or "the Pond." Wright maintained a tavern and frequently held barbecues, music festivals, and other events to increase the business in his tavern.

Between 1823 and 1826, racing meets were held on private racing tracks around Lexington, including Henry Clay's Ashland Farm.

Another track during this period was at Fowler's Garden. Opened by 1817 by Captain John Fowler, a local businessman, it lay on the east side of Lexington. Local historian Randolph Hollingsworth says it was about twenty-five acres in size. J. Winston Coleman, on the other hand, asserts it covered between fifty and seventy-five acres. Both agree that it had a racetrack, stables, and related buildings, as well as facilities for fairs, livestock shows, political rallies, entertainments, and exhibits "of all kinds." Hollingsworth locates the Garden between Main and Fifth Streets (south and north) and Walton Avenue on the east in to Race Street on the west. Being on the east edge of town, it was more accessible than the Williams track and became the social center of Lexington, one writer describing it as the "fashionable Country Club of its day," with dinners and dances in the Garden. The Town Branch flowed through the property as well and that the community celebrated the fiftieth anniversary of American independence there. Fowler's Garden closed around 1860.

In April 1826, members of the old Jockey Club met at Mrs. Keene's Inn to start a new racing association. They entered into a subscription agreement to capitalize the new entity and agreed to conduct a preparatory race meet that June. Sixty subscribers paid fifty dollars each for one share in the new Kentucky Association for the Improvement of the Breeds of Domestic Stock. On June 8, a three-day meet began running over the old Lexington Course. The race the first day was a three-mile run, the second day a two miler, and the third day over one mile, with the horse carrying the best of the three wins as the purse winner. The third day also saw a handicap race. Over a great distance, age and weight carried mattered little; but on a shorter course, different weights (typically lead bars in saddle bags) were assigned according to the age of the horses.

The Kentucky Association held its August race meet in 1826 at the Williams track, and racing appears to have continued there through 1830, but it also appears clear that the association intended from the start to develop a new track under its ownership.

The reason for that decision is not clear. It could simply be a desire to own the land. There does not seem to have been any disagreement with the owners of the Williams tract, as racing there was permitted for four years. There may have been some geographic shortcoming or defect in course design, but in any event, it appears the search for a new site began early.

On July 7, 1828, the association purchased more than fifty acres from John Postlethwaite on the northeastern edge of town, at the east end of Fifth Street, close to the northernmost platted street. This site would be much more accessible to the residents of Lexington. The purchase was an "insider" transaction, as it would be known today, since John Postlethwaite was both the seller (with his wife) and a member of the board of trustees for the association. However, his ownership was publicly known, and the price must have been fair for the other trustees to agree.

A week later, on July 15, the association purchased all or a part of Out Lot 18 within the city limits. Described as 20 poles by 40 poles, the lot was 330 feet by 660 feet at the south end of town and lay the entire length of Lexington from the new track site. The intended use of the lot is unknown, and Ambrose does not mention it. In the Lexington platting scheme, small In Lots were clustered around the commons and were intended for residences, while the Out Lots were intended, at least at first, to be agricultural, where residents would grow crops or keep stock. The Town Branch flowed through the lot, and perhaps it was intended as pasture and corral for horses coming to race.

That summer construction began on the new one-mile oval track laid out in a modern flat design. The spring of 1829 saw the first races. A grandstand was erected in the center of the infield the following year, offering a view of the entire track, and the first formal meet was held in 1831. Admittance to the track was free, but admittance to the grandstand (and no doubt the reason for placing it in the infield) cost twenty-five cents.

In 1834, an adjoining ten-acre parcel was purchased for the track, and in July 1836, four more acres were added, bringing the area to more than sixty-five acres. The association enclosed the entire property with a wood plank fence.

The location of the Kentucky Association race rack would have been just east or north east of Fowler's Garden, and Hollingsworth implies that the KA track became the focus of horse races, while the Garden stopped races and focused more on being the community entertainment center and fairgrounds.

Racing continued at the Kentucky Association Course through 1898, including one meet held while the Confederate army occupied Lexington, but a national financial panic, the opening of competing tracks, and financial problems caused the track to close. For several years, crops were grown in the infield, and certain trainers leased the track as a training facility. In October 1903, Captain Samuel S. Brown from Pittsburgh purchased the property and began a series of improvements. The first grandstand was torn down to open the infield, as were many sheds and outbuildings along the back side. A new grandstand with a two-thousand-spectator capacity was built along (and outside) the home stretch, and the clubhouse was substantially renovated. A new paddock barn with fourteen stalls was added as well as a "betting shed," which had stations for up to sixty bookmakers—at the time a legal activity outside the city limits.

The moribund association revived and held its first race—a six-day meet—at the new facility in May 1905.

By 1907, Brown had died, and the association, newly reorganized, purchased the property from his estate. Admission was one dollar for gentlemen and half that for ladies; daily programs were ten cents. The next year, the pari-mutuel wagering system was introduced to the track.

Racing continued into the 1930s, but financial pressures resulting from the Great Depression forced the track's closure, with the last race run in 1932. Negotiations over several months resulted. In 1935, the federal government purchased the land for just over $67,000 for use as a housing project, and buildings and equipment were auctioned to the public.

KEENELAND RACE COURSE

Almost immediately upon the closing of the Kentucky Association track, horsemen began looking for a site for a new track. J.O. "Jack" Keene had spent years trying to build a private racetrack and clubhouse on his farm on the Versailles Road, with limited success. In 1933, the newly formed Keeneland Association purchased over 147 acres from Keene and began converting his private facilities into a public track.

On October 11, 1936, the association held an open house to introduce the public to its track and its new Totalizator tote board, or bet and odds tracking displays. Opening day for the Fall Meet was October 15, 1936, and first day attendance was 25,337 race fans.

Improvements and changes marked the next several years. A new box seat area was constructed for the Spring 1950 Meet, and the original wooden grandstand was replaced by one of steel and concrete. Three years later, the grandstand was enlarged, adding over 1,500 seats, and the finish line was repositioned, extending the course length.

Keeneland. *Peter Brackney.*

In 1961, an alphanumeric message board was added in front of the tote board, and later that year, a new timer display showing race fractions and final race finish time was also added. Two years later, an alternate finish line was established. During the 1970s, Keeneland erected five new barns.

On October 11, 1984, Queen Elizabeth II attended the races at Keeneland. In her honor, Keeneland established the Queen Elizabeth II Challenge Cup race for fillies and mares. She presented the trophy to the winner in a newly constructed Winner's Circle.

Two years later, the track was awarded National Historic Landmark status by the U.S. Department of the Interior.

A significant event happened at the Spring Meet in 1997. For the first time, Keeneland races were called by a track announcer over a public address system. Prior thereto, Keeneland was the only track in the country not to have an on-track announcer. In a major coup for Keeneland, it was chosen to host the Breeders' Cup Races in 2015. The track and supporters in the community responded so well that the Breeders' Cup Races returned in 2020.

THE RED MILE AND FLORAL HALL

Kentucky's first organized trotting horse entity, the Kentucky Trotting Horse Breeders Association, was started in 1859. It purchased land where the University of Kentucky student center complex stands now. It built a track and viewing stands there and held the first meets in 1859, 1860, and 1861. However, the site was occupied by the Union army as a camp. At some point prior to the end of the Civil War, the grandstand burned. The federal government paid the association $25,000 in damages, and that money was used to purchase replacement land off South Broadway for a new fairgrounds and track.

After the war, the Kentucky Agricultural & Mechanical Association established fairgrounds on what is now the Red Mile property. Beginning in 1875, the fairgrounds were leased by the Trotting Association for race meets and has been in continuous use as such since, making the Red Mile the second-oldest trotting track in the United States and the oldest in Kentucky. It hosts one leg of the Triple Crown of Harness Racing, the annual Kentucky Futurity.

In 1882, famous Lexington architect John McMurty designed and built Floral Hall at the edge of the Red Mile track. It was built to house

Floral Hall. *Foster Ockerman Jr.*

floral exhibits and contests during fairs. The interior was on three levels around an open center atrium. Racks were arranged in tiers so flowers could be displayed easily and the judges could assess the competition in a 360-degree view.

Floral Hall was just outside the city limits of Lexington in the early days of racing, and the bookkeepers set up shop when bookkeeping was outlawed in the town. (In like fashion, the old Kentucky Association Track's clubhouse and finish line were inside the city limits, while the bookkeeper sheds were located down the stretch outside the limits.)

The Trotting Association took over ownership of the fairgrounds in 1896, creating the modern Red Mile track. Floral Hall was converted to stables. Horses were stalled on the first and second floors, and the grooms slept on the third floor. During World War I, the hall was converted to army barracks.

In 1960, a new foundation, the Stable of Memories Inc., was started to take control of and manage Floral Hall. It raised funds in the community to restore the building. The upper floors contain a museum of trots-related items, and the ground floor can be leased for events.

EQUINE CEMETERIES

According to Thoroughbred Heritage, there are at least 165 equine cemeteries and graves in Kentucky, several on private farms around Lexington.

One of the largest is on the famous Calumet Farm outside Lexington, where, as of 2014, there were sixty-three gravestones. The stallion Bull Lea's monument is centered on the tree-lined area. His seven winning colts are buried and marked in a semicircle in front of him. In another semicircle are

Hamburg Equine Cemetery. *Foster Ockerman Jr.*

his daughters who produced Kentucky Derby winners. Other grave markers are to the left and right.

Another famous equine cemetery (and one easily accessed as it is adjacent to a public street) is the Hamburg Place Cemetery; it is one of the oldest dedicated to horses. John E. Madden developed Hamburg Place farm starting with 235 acres he purchased in 1897 with the proceeds from selling the racehorse Hamburg. The farm eventually grew to 2,300 contiguous acres.

Madden was a top trainer and breeder in the early twentieth century, breeding not only Thoroughbreds but standardbreds and ponies as well. Among many others, he had five Kentucky Derby winners, one Triple Crown winner, and four Belmont Stakes winners.

He created the first equine cemetery on the farm in 1908. Beginning in 2005, the farm has been developed commercially into a regional shopping center, residential, and commercial and office areas. The widening of Winchester Road made relocating the cemetery necessary. The streets in the development are all named after famous Hamburg Place horses, and the relocated cemetery is on Sir Barton Way, named for Sir Barton, the first Triple Crown winner. Eighteen horses are buried in the cemetery.

CARRIAGE RACING AND THE MCDOWELL SPEEDWAY

Before there were four-wheeled vehicles powered by engines racing around NASCAR speedways, there were four-wheeled carriages pulled by horses in races called speedways. Carriage races were not popular in the pioneer era in Kentucky for the lack of good roads, but with the advent of large oval racetracks with level surfaces and paved roads, they became more frequent.

By the turn of the twentieth century, there was the League of Amateur Driving Clubs, with local clubs in many cities, including Boston, New York City, Syracuse, Pittsburgh, Chicago, Detroit, Memphis, and Lexington.

As early as 1872, match races were held on Lexington's tracks. The 1904 summer Horse Show and Matinee Race meeting included "two speedway rings." The events were open only to members of the Driving Club, and a total of sixteen silver julep cups were awarded.

At this time, another significant trend was underway and would lead to a most unusual speedway. For decades, under state law, while a city maintained its streets, roads outside the city limits had been licensed or franchised to private toll road companies. In the later part of the nineteenth century, there was a movement to authorize the private companies to sell their interests to the government. On July 23, 1897, the Fayette County Fiscal Court (the county's governing body) met to discuss buying three roads—the Richmond, Georgetown, and Nicholasville pikes—with the goal of making travel free of tolls. While the acquisition of the other roads was comparatively uneventful, Richmond Road's acquisition took an interesting turn.

Carriage race start at the Red Mile. *From the Lexington Leader.*

In 1882, Major Henry Clay McDowell and his wife, Ann Clay, daughter of Henry Clay Jr., purchased the 324-acre former Henry Clay estate with an eye to restoring it, both house and grounds. McDowell enjoyed racing carriages.

In August 1897, McDowell purchased a fifty-foot-wide strip of land on the other side of Richmond Road, running from the city limits two miles out along and beside Richmond Road to a lake. He then deeded the land to the county under the conditions that it construct an improved dirt road level with the existing road, that no streetcar or railroad were to be put in it, and the county would repair or replace farm fences taken down in the process. The new roadway was so constructed as to leave a string of parkways between the two courses—in effect, creating an infield for McDowell's carriage races. By the following spring, the newly improved way became a "pleasure drive" to carriages and trotting horses out to the lake. Carriage races with matched teams of horses were held along this speedway with crowds gathering to watch the finish. A Chicago newspaper called it "one of the best drives of its kind in the country." The county contracted for it to be harrowed and worked in the summer "until it is almost as fast as a regulation track."

McDowell died in 1899. The following spring, H.H. Gratz, heir of Benjamin Gratz, for whom Gratz Park is named, appeared before the county fiscal court to request that the boulevard be known as the H.C. McDowell Speedway and a monument erected recognizing McDowell's key role in the roadway improvements. The request was approved, and a monument was erected. Between residential developments and road widening, the exact location has moved a couple of times. It currently sits on the parkway in the middle of Richmond Road near the Henry Clay Estate of Ashland.

THE HOMES OF KENTUCKY BASKETBALL

Before there was Rupp Arena, there was Memorial Coliseum. Before there was Memorial Coliseum, there was the Alumni Gym. Before there was the Alumni Gym, well, there really wasn't basketball.

The University of Kentucky was a football school. Extensive fundraising and the construction of a new football field and stadium along Euclid Avenue occupied the interests of students and community alike. Basketball, such as it was, was barely more than an intermural sport; if not for the teams from Transylvania University across town and Centre College in Danville to provide local rivalries, basketball might have remained a minor sport. Basketball was played in the Buell Armorry where there was limited standing room for observers.

But in 1923, the Alumni Association began lobbying for a new gymnasium over the financial objections of the university administration. Eventually, the funds were raised, and Alumni Gym was completed in time for the 1924–25 season. The gym was sited, and still stands, on Euclid Avenue near Limestone. The original basketball facility held all of 2,800 spectators, but it was a significant increase in seats and quality of facility over the armory. Today, Alumni Gym has been reconstructed and remodeled into a fitness center for the university community and integrated into the enlarged and remodeled student center.

During the time Wildcats played in the gym from 1924 to 1950, they played 287 games and lost only 25, including the six years before Adolph Rupp arrived on the scene.

When Dr. H.L. Donovan became the new president of the university in 1941, he arrived with a plan for a new physical education building "that will properly take care of our athletics." The intervention of World War II delayed pursuing that plan, but the postwar influx of students returned the importance of new athletic facilities.

Alumni Gym. *Foster Ockerman Jr.*

Memorial Coliseum. *Foster Ockerman Jr.*

Memorial Coliseum, also placed along Euclid Avenue, was completed in 1950 at a cost of almost $4 million as a memorial to the more than 10,000 Kentuckians who died in World War II and the Korean conflict. The original seating capacity was 11,500, another significant increase in fan capacity over Alumni Gym. Renovations in 1990 reduced seating to 8,500 but added weight-training facilities, new coaches' offices, a players' lounge, and other features. It houses the University Athletics offices and is home to women's basketball, volleyball, and gymnastics.

But beginning in the 1960s, ticket sales for men's basketball was closed to the public. Season ticket holders and the student seating allotment soaked up all of the 11,500 seats. Agitation began for yet another basketball facility.

At the same time, Lexington was in the process of re-creating its downtown. Funds from the federal Urban Renewal Program allowed for the purchase of railroad right of way and the removal of tracks from downtown. At its greatest expansion by the railroads, as many as eight tracks lay in what today is the Vine Street corridor. Warehouses associated with the railroads also came down, and the corridor was replanned to facilitate modern urban development.

A civic center was integral to these plans, originally intended to span from High to Main Streets, crossing over the new Vine Street, between Upper and Mill Streets. This plan fell apart when a local bank bought one of the intended blocks for a new bank and office building and parking garage. With the removal of the Louisville & Nashville Railroad's switching yard west of Broadway in the Town Branch Valley, attention shifted to that site.

Debate raged across the university campus and the community about whether it was a good thing for the basketball arena to be off-campus. Because of the natural bowl effect of the area, Main and High Streets were three and four stories respectively above grade, and there was even some talk of building a new football stadium as well as a basketball arena in the area. Eventually, the university decided to place the new football stadium and related facilities on its former farm on Cooper Drive.

But the convention center plans for a 60,000-square-foot convention facility and three-story shopping mall moved forward, to which was added a basketball arena with an official capacity of 23,500 seats but could swell to accommodate over 24,000 fans at times due to bleacher seating in the upper arena. A 2019 renovation that added seatbacks to the upper arena reduced capacity to just over 20,000.

The arena was named after longtime successful basketball coach Adolph Rupp. It opened in 1976, slightly more than a year before Coach Rupp's death in 1977.

ISAAC MURPHY MEMORIAL ART GARDEN

Isaac Murphy's birth year is in dispute, varying between 1856 and 1864. Even whether he was born free or enslaved is in doubt. What is not doubted is that Murphy was one of the best thoroughbred jockeys. His lifetime win percentage of 44 percent has never been surpassed. He was the first jockey to ride consecutive Kentucky Derby winners and was the first rider to win three Derbies. At one time, he was the leader of what has come to be called America's first professional athlete class. He and his wife bought a house on Third Street near Midland Avenue. It had a rooftop balcony area where he could watch the horses exercise and race at the Kentucky Association Track. When the National Museum of Racing and Hall of Fame was established in 1955, Murphy was the first jockey inducted.

The Isaac Murphy Memorial Art Garden has been located on the site of Murphy's former house, honoring him and the early African American jockeys.

THE KENTUCKY HORSE PARK

The Kentucky Horse Park is a unique feature. At 1,224 acres, it is the largest equine-themed park in the world, dedicated to "man's relationship with the horse." It is both an educational park and a working horse farm. It showcases all breeds of horse through daily presentations and a parade of breeds, three horse-related museums, horse-drawn carriage tours, an art gallery, horseback riding, pony rides, and special exhibitions. And all of this is just on a daily basis. There are frequent horse shows and competitions in steeplechase over its custom course, cross-country competitions, polo, and the only four-star equestrian event in North America: the Kentucky Three Day Event. In 2010, the Horse Park became the first North American host for the FEI World Equestrian Games, which was the largest sporting event of any kind ever held in Kentucky with over 500,000 spectators watching over 800 athletes. More than 900 horses from 60 countries competed. Owned by the Commonwealth of Kentucky, the Horse Park is run by a separate nonprofit corporation.

The park also is the location of the National Horse Center. This center is the headquarters for over thirty national, regional, and state equine organizations. The list includes the American Association of Equine Practitioners, American Hackney Horse Society, American Hanoverian Society, American Saddlebred Horse Association, Carriage Association of America, and the United States Hunter/Jumper Association.

The Rolex Stadium is a 7,338-seat outdoor stadium that can be expanded with the addition of temporary bleachers to an almost 38,000-person capacity for larger horse shows, concerts, and other outdoor events. Set up for concerts, capacity is nearly 52,000 persons, making this stadium the largest concert venue in central Kentucky.

The Alltech Arena complements the stadium as an indoor arena seating up to 8,500. The arena floor measures 135 feet by 300 feet and can accommodate horse shows and rodeos of a variety of natures. The concourse has 50,000 square feet of space and is host to a range of nonequestrian events such as the Kentucky Book Festival.

Historically, the Horse Park sits in what was originally a nine-thousand-acre land grant by the Commonwealth of Virginia to Colonel William Christian for service in the French and Indian War. Christian and his family moved to Kentucky County, Virginia, in 1785. (Statehood was not until 1792.) Upon his death at the hands of Indians in 1786, his daughter Elizabeth inherited some three thousand acres in Fayette and Scott Counties, including what is now the park. The land changed hands several times until a sale to S.J. Salyers, who built the house in 1866. It is now used for Horse Park administrative offices. In 1897, another owner built the training track, which is still in use today by the park.

Again, a succession of owners—some as purchasers, some as heirs, some buying at public auction—continued to improve the farm with water towers drawing from an ever-flowing spring, barns, and other improvements. Finally, in 1972, the Commonwealth of Kentucky purchased the farm for the Horse Park, which opened to the public in 1978.

As if all this were not enough, the Horse Park is home to three equine museums. The International Museum of the Horse, a Smithsonian affiliate, examines the role of horses throughout world history from the most ancient times. It has both a permanent exhibit and periodic special exhibits and a collection of equine art. The American Saddlebred Museum focuses on the saddlebred horse in American history and culture. It has both a large library and exhibits. The Wheeler Museum focuses on show jumpers and has a collection of equestrian memorabilia ranging from antique tack and equipment to trophies and photographs.

4

HISTORIC NEIGHBORHOODS OF LEXINGTON

In 1955, the Hart-Bradford House at the southwest corner of Second and Mill Streets was demolished to make way for a parking lot. The historic two-and-one-half story house had been the home of figures significant to Lexington's history, including Thomas Hart (early settler and entrepreneur whose daughter, Lucretia, married Henry Clay in the home's parlor), John Bradford (a Renaissance man who had his hand in almost every venture in Lexington, usually with success), and Laura Clay (suffragist and first woman to have her name placed for nomination to be U.S. president at a major political party convention). The demolition of this historic home had a significant and permanent effect on the preservation of Lexington's tangible history. First, the group that became the Blue Grass Trust for Historic Preservation was organized in an effort to save Hopemont, the Hunt-Morgan House, across Second Street. The second major effect was that the Gratz Park neighborhood became the city's first historic district in 1958.

Historic zoning overlays protect significant structures and spaces within their bounds from construction, demolition, or exterior renovation that might adversely affect the historic qualities of the neighborhood. These kinds of ordinances are powerful tools for those who seek to preserve history. Since Gratz Park was declared Lexington's first historic district, fourteen other districts have been established. Two historic landmarks (St. Paul A.M.E. Church and Helm Place) have also been designated for protection under the local ordinances.

ASHLAND PARK

Ashland Park, consisting of nearly 190 acres, became a historic district in 2013. The neighborhood is named after Ashland, the home of Henry Clay. That landmark stands in the neighborhood's eastern edge. There are approximately 505 contributing buildings in the district, with several architectural styles represented, including Craftsman, Tudor Revival, Prairie, Colonial Revival, and Bungalow. Nearly all of the early twentieth-century buildings are residences—few have been converted to other purposes.

The initial phase of the Ashland Park development was laid out by the Brookline, Massachusetts firm Olmsted Brothers, whose founder laid out New York City's Central Park. Olmsted's layout of Ashland Park is distinctive and unique among Lexington's neighborhoods.

AYLESFORD

The Aylesford historic district lies to the east of Lexington's downtown core. It is largely residential. Many of its historic homes have been converted into housing for students at the nearby University of Kentucky. Other homes and businesses surround Woodland Park, once the site of the Agricultural College of the Kentucky University, later the University of Kentucky.

The home of Senator John Pope and his wife, Eliza, was designed by Benjamin Henry Latrobe. It is one of only a few Latrobe-designed residences remaining in the country. *Peter Brackney*.

On the western edge of the Aylesford District lies Pope Villa, the home of Senator John Pope and his wife, Eliza. It was designed in 1810–11 by Benjamin Henry Latrobe, who was one of the most significant architects of that time in the United States. Few of Latrobe's residential designs remain today, and the design of Pope Villa is unique: it is "a perfect square, with a domed, circular rotunda in the center of the second story." Latrobe was significantly involved in the design and construction of both the White House and the Capitol in Washington, D.C.

The Aylesford historic district was established in 1998.

BELL COURT

Bell Court was laid out at the dawn of the twentieth century. Among the Queen Anne, Romanesque, Arts and Craft, and Colonial residences, however, are two mansions which predate the neighborhood.

Bell Place, the heart of Bell Court, was constructed on the foundation of Woodside. Woodside was designed by local architect Thomas Lewinski for Henry Bell on thirty-five acres of land that Bell had acquired from Colonel John Todd. On a visit to the Bell's former home on the site, Mary Todd Lincoln wrote to her mother that "the house and grounds are magnificent." Henry Bell's residence burned in 1884. After the fire, Bell Place was built without any concern of cost overruns.

The other historic mansion in Bell Court is Clay Villa. It was also designed by Thomas Lewinski around 1846. Henry Clay commissioned the

Bell Place is the magnificent centerpiece of the Bell Court Historic District. *Peter Brackney.*

design of Clay Villa for his son James. When the Great Compromiser died the following decade, James demolished the original Ashland and had the present structure rebuilt on the old foundation.

The Episcopal Church of the Good Shepherd also lies within the Bell Court neighborhood. Reverend Thomas Settle was an outspoken critic of a bill in Frankfort that would have banned pari-mutuel gambling and even spoke before the legislature. With the minister's strong voice against the proposal, it failed by one vote. Over the next few years, nearly $200,000 was raised by horsemen for the purpose of erecting a new church as an expression of gratitude to Reverend Settle.

CADENTOWN

In 1867, Owen Caden purchased land east of Lexington in Fayette County. Caden, a farmer who immigrated to the United States in 1840, sought to provide housing to former slaves. The area around Cadentown has been significantly developed since the historic district was established in 2001, and were it not for the designation, it is almost certain that any tangible remain of this post–Civil War African American hamlet would have been lost.

The primary structures in Cadentown are the Baptist church and the old Cadentown School. The school served the community from 1922 until 1947; its basic design followed the Rosenwald standard. Julius Rosenwald (1862–1932) was a native of Springfield, Illinois, and a friend of the Lincoln family who became the president of the Sears, Roebuck and Company. The

The Cadentown School served this African American hamlet in eastern Fayette County from 1922 until 1947. *Library of Congress.*

store's famed mail-order catalogue was Rosenwald's idea. His relationship with Booker T. Washington led him to give considerable sums toward the education of rural African Americans. With his help, over three hundred schools were established in three states, including the school at Cadentown.

Cadentown was once one of thirty hamlets for freed slaves in the Bluegrass established after the Civil War. Of this number, few are intact. Cadentown's first lot was sold in 1869, and all were transferred within ten years; lots ranged from one to eight acres. The historic Cadentown Baptist Church was established in 1879 and has a cemetery.

CONSTITUTION

Constitution Historic District is often referred to as Lexington's first subdivision, having been developed in the 1810s. The district lies behind the federal courthouse past Third Street, extending from North Limestone in the west to Martin Luther King Boulevard in the east. There are fifty-four buildings in the primarily residential area. The two most significant houses in Constitution are the Weir House (312 North Limestone) and the Matthew Kennedy House (216 North Limestone).

James Weir was a prominent merchant heavily involved in the region's important hemp industry. He also served as a founding member of the Lexington & Ohio Railroad. Weir had this two-story Greek Revival built in 1822. The design is attributed to Gideon Shryock, though another builder (John McMurtry) likely completed the structure. The foundation and latrine were dug by "King" Solomon, who would later help bury many of those who perished in the local cholera outbreaks. It is said that King Solomon was immune to the disease because he drank liquor, not water. The house is commonly now known as the Carrick House after the family who lived there from 1910 to 1954; it is today utilized as a banquet facility.

The Matthew Kennedy House today houses a shop called Mulberry & Lime; the name honors the street's two historic names (Mulberry and Limestone). Matthew Kennedy was the first in Kentucky to adopt the "architect" title; his most significant works included buildings on Transylvania's campus. (The main building was completed in 1818 but burned in 1829, and the medical hall, completed in 1827, burned in 1839.)

Although primarily residential, the Limestone corridor includes many commercial buildings that were constructed in the latter half of the 1800s. Another residence on the Limestone corridor was converted long ago into

Above: The Weir House was built in 1822. It is today known as the Carrick House after the family who lived there from 1910 until 1954. *University of Kentucky Libraries.*

Left: Sayre School on Lexington's North Limestone Street was established in 1856. *University of Kentucky Libraries.*

a school. John McMurtry added a third floor and the iconic cupola to the original 1846 Thomas Lewinski design. David Sayre, a silversmith and proprietor of the first private bank in Lexington, founded Sayre School in 1856 "to further the education of young ladies."

ELSMERE PARK

Established as a historic district overlay in 1976, Elsmere Park was one of Lexington's first planned suburban neighborhoods. It was laid out in 1890 by the Elsmere Park Company just off North Broadway between Sixth and Seventh Streets. Its T-shaped cul-de-sac design gives a sense of privacy.

Houses on Elsmere Park were built between 1891 and 1913 for professors and other professionals. The first house on the street was Jefferson House (1891) at 645 Elsmere Park and was home to a University of Kentucky professor, Samuel M. Jefferson. In 1902, the president of the Elsmere Park Company, George H. Whitney, built the street's first frame residence as a wedding gift for his daughter and her husband. Until the Whitney House, all homes on Elsmere were constructed of brick in the Romanesque style. Other homes built after the Whitney House were more varied in architectural style. Altogether, the twenty-nine residences on the street reflect the shift in style that occurred in the decades on either side of the beginning of the twentieth century.

FAYETTE PARK

Nine years after Elsmere Park became a historic district, Fayette Park received the same status. And like Elsmere Park, Fayette Park is a cul-de-sac planned neighborhood. Fayette Park, however, predates Elsmere Park, albeit only slightly. It was laid out in 1888 and 1889 and is located on a block closer to town and on the opposite side of North Broadway from Elsmere.

Fayette Park's cul-de-sac includes a central landscaped island. Many of the homes are also in the Romanesque style, which was common in the era. Early residents included Reverend John McGarvey (442 Fayette Park), who served as the College of the Bible's president. That college ultimately became the foundation for Lexington Theological Seminary. Another local minister, Reverend Mark Collis of Broadway Christian Church, had the Richardsonian home at 438 Fayette Park built for his family. Noted horseman

Residences in the Fayette Park Historic District. *University of Kentucky Libraries.*

Hart Boswell owned 423 Fayette Park from its completion in 1889 until he sold it in 1927 to distinguished attorney and historian Samuel M. Wilson. Wilson's papers were contributed to the University of Kentucky and became the foundation for the university's special collections department. Another resident was Daniel Swigert, the noted horseman who named Elmendorf Farm and bred Kentucky Derby winners Hindoo (1881), Apollo (1882), and Ben Ali (1886).

GRATZ PARK

Clay Lancaster, a Kentucky native and an authority on American architecture, said that Gratz Park "has charm, atmosphere, a sense of tranquility and of history, and it provides an oasis of planting tucked into the cityscape." Its history is filled with names of prominent Bluegrass families like Hunt, Morgan, Hart, Gratz, Bodley, Dudley, Woolley, and Roberts.

Gratz Park was Lexington's first historic district, achieving that landmark status in 1958. It is bounded by Lexington's Third, Mill, Second, and Market Streets. On its ground once stood Transylvania Seminary's three-story main

Mount Hope, the home of Benjamin Gratz, is located at Mill and New Streets. Gratz Park, an oasis in the city, is named for him. *Peter Brackney*.

A statue called *The Fountain of Youth* was given to the City of Lexington by author James Lane Allen. Located in Gratz Park, Transylvania University's Old Morrison is visible in the background. *Peter Brackney*.

building. But an 1829 fire destroyed that building, leading Transylvania to retreat across Third Street. The Old Kitchen Building, however, remains standing on the east side of the park, dating to Transylvania's presence on the south side of Third Street. Townhouses from the 1800s surround the park named for Lexington business and civic leader Benjamin Gratz. Gratz's home, Mount Hope, stands at the corner of Mill and New Streets.

A gift to the "children of Lexington"—a fountain statue called *The Fountain of Youth*—was made by author James Lane Allen in his will. On the opposite end of the park from the fountain is the Carnegie Library (now the Carnegie Center for Literacy and Learning), which was constructed in 1906 from funds donated by steel magnate Andrew Carnegie. Lexington once had two Carnegie libraries, but the other—once on the campus of the University of Kentucky—was demolished in the 1960s. The Lexington Public Library was housed at Gratz Park from 1906 until 1989, when its central branch opened on Main Street at the site of the old Phoenix Hotel.

MULBERRY HILL

Mulberry Street no longer exists in Lexington, though it was once one of the city's most important thoroughfares. It was renamed Limestone Street in 1887. Two of the most significant residents of Mulberry Hill lived at 343 North Limestone. It is believed that a portion of the house was built for Adam Rankin in 1797; Rankin sold the residence to John Bell in 1817. Rankin was a minister in Lexington's early Presbyterian Church. He formed Presbyterian congregations in Jessamine County (Ebenezer), Woodford County (Pisgah and Glenn's Creek), and Fayette County (Mount Zion). Rankin was a disagreeable sort who had ongoing conflict with the Transylvania Presbytery. Ultimately, he was disassociated in 1792. The house at 343 North Limestone is among the oldest in Lexington, but another house associated with Rankin may be the oldest. His circa 1784 home at 317 South Mill Street (relocated from High Street in the 1970s, it became the home of the Lexington History Museum in 2020) is considered the oldest in the city. John Bell, who acquired 343 North Limestone from Rankin in 1817, represented Kentucky at the state constitutional conventions in Danville. He also served as an early representative from Fayette County in the newly formed Kentucky House of Representatives.

Lord Morton's house at 530 North Limestone Street lies in the middle of Duncan Park just to the north of the Mulberry Hill district. Even so,

Lord Morton's House at the heart of Duncan Park. Morton was an important merchant in Lexington, as well as a philanthropist. *Peter Brackney*.

it is an important property and included on walking tours of the district. Morton was a significant merchant in early Lexington with shops along the first block of South Upper Street. (These were demolished in 2008.) Morton was a significant philanthropist and gave large sums to the city's Episcopal churches as well as to the city for the cause of public education. After Morton's death in 1836, the property was sold to Cassius Marcellus Clay, who published a newspaper, the *True American*, while living here. The newspaper was a leading abolitionist publication for which Clay received much opposition. Later, former mayor Henry Duncan (for whom Duncan Park is named) owned the home. The city acquired the property, considered one of the finest of Lexington's early town residences, and land in 1913.

NORTHSIDE

The Northside Historic District includes many areas that fill the spaces between other districts like the Western Suburb, Elsmere and Fayette Parks, and Mulberry Hill. Some of these other areas are incorporated into the Northside Historic Residential District, which was added to the National Register of Historic Places in 1970. A neighborhood association follows the boundaries of the National Register listing, which includes forty city blocks and approximately 1,700 structures. The expansive geography—from Newtown Pike to Limestone Street and from Church Street to just beyond Seventh Street—lends itself to much diversity in architectural styles, historical communities, and socioeconomic classes.

A good example of this diversity can be found on the parallel streets of Ross Avenue and Hampton Court. The latter was developed shortly before World War I as an urban cul-de-sac surrounded by stone walls and arched entries. Built on the site of an old orphan asylum, the beautiful homes and luxury apartments of Hampton Court enjoy a central park-like area in the heart of downtown. Contrast this with Ross Avenue, which was built around the same time. Most of the houses on this road are nearly identical one-story T-plan houses that would have housed lower-middle-class professionals in the neighborhood's heyday.

The arched stone entrance to Hampton Court in Lexington's Northside. *Peter Brackney.*

African American enclaves in the Northside neighborhood grew along College, Henry, and Miller Streets; other urban clusters like Brucetown, Goodloetown, and Taylortown arose in Lexington as the city became more segregated. Many areas of the Northside are being redeveloped.

One example of this commercial redevelopment is the reimagination of the old Rainbo Bread Company building at Jefferson and Sixth Streets. The oldest part of the building was constructed as the Holsum Bread Company in the 1890s; subsequent renovations kept the bread factory going until it closed in the early 1990s. Today, it is the home of the West Sixth Brewing Company.

SEVEN PARKS

Of the fifteen historic zoning overlays in Lexington, Seven Parks is one of the farthest from downtown (only Cadentown is farther). Seven Parks lies on either side of Nicholasville Road and includes properties on Nicholasville Road, Barberry Lane, Arcadia Park, Elizabeth Street, Dantzler Court, Dantzler Drive, and Shawnee Place. To the east, it is bordered by railroad tracks.

The historic district was developed in the early to mid-1900s as a middle-class neighborhood consisting of mostly one- and one-half-story houses largely in the Colonial Revival and Tudor Revival styles. When constructed, these properties were located outside of the city limits but were annexed in the 1950s. In 1997, the approximately two hundred homes of Seven Parks were given the historic district status by the city.

SOUTH ASHLAND/CENTRAL AVENUE

This historic district, established in 1989, largely includes properties along South Ashland; the Ashland Park district is truly an extension to the south and east of this earlier district. The mansions on South Ashland create one of Lexington's most beautiful streets.

The opulent houses here were constructed in the late nineteenth and early twentieth centuries. The area was annexed into the city in 1908, kicking off a major debate: "Shall Ashland Avenue be macadamized and made into a street or remain a pike?" According to the *Lexington Leader*, "Bitter feeling is said to exist among the neighbors and one of the strongest fights ever waged before Council is expected." The debate did not conclude for months; ultimately, the road was paved.

SOUTH HILL

On Lexington's original 1781 plat, what became South Hill consisted of Out Lots K–Q; today, it is bounded largely by South Limestone, High, South Broadway, and Pine Streets. Appropriately, the district is named because the five-acre Out Lots were located on a hill on the south side of Lexington. From this hill, you could view the Town Branch flowing through the city. Structures in the neighborhood were built beginning in the early 1800s and continued to develop over the next century.

The city's earliest surviving home, the Adam Rankin House, is located on South Mill Street in the district, although its original location was on West High Street. Farther south on Mill Street lies the Dudley School, which was named for benefactor Dr. Benjamin W. Dudley, a surgeon from Transylvania University. Dudley School opened elsewhere in 1851, and the present building was completed in 1881 in in the Italianate style. Today, it is the home to shops and restaurants.

On South Limestone, the Oldham House represents an important part of Lexington's African American story. It was built around 1835 by Samuel and Daphney Oldham. In 1826, Samuel Oldham was enslaved but purchased his own freedom over the course of a year. He became a business owner with a barbershop on Main Street; he was also an unofficial attorney for the city's free Black community. By 1830, he purchased the freedom of his wife, Daphney, and their sons. A freed family, they built the two-story, five-bay common bond brick house.

The former Presbyterian mission turned synagogue discussed later in this book located at 120 West Maxwell Street served religious communities from 1891 until 1986. Another church in the district is the First United Methodist Church at 200 West High. The congregation constructed a house of worship on what was then called Hill Street in 1842 but replaced it with the present Neoclassical Revival sanctuary in 1907.

When South Hill was added to the National Register in 1978, the area was described as "a pocket of urbanity not yet eroded by the ravages of time and neglect nor engulfed by commercial development." New investment in the area has begun to alter the neighborhood, but it remains largely intact, and investment in the area has helped to restore once-dilapidated structures like the Oldham House.

WESTERN SUBURB

The Western Suburb was platted in 1815 (making it Lexington's first suburb) on land once owned by Colonel John Todd. Colonel Todd was a Revolutionary War officer who was killed at the Battle of Blue Licks. His daughter, Mary Owen Todd, inherited all of her father's vast estate, making her the richest woman in Kentucky at the age of three years old. The suburb's houses were built alongside the residents' varied businesses and trades. Carpentry shops, blacksmith shops, liveries, and coal and lumber yards were located throughout the neighborhood.

One of the Western Suburb's most infamous residents was madam Belle Brezing. Born in 1860, Belle lived a difficult early life before being taken in by Jennie Hill. Hill operated what was then the finest brothel "house" in town, and it was located in the house known today as the Mary Todd Lincoln House. The Mary Todd Lincoln House lies just outside the historic Western Suburb's boundaries and is a worthy destination. Buddy Thompson wrote in his biography of Brezing that she raised prostitution "to an art form" before

The 600 block of West Short Street runs through the heart of the Western Historic Suburb. *Peter Brackney.*

Above: First Baptist Church on Main Street in Lexington stands on the site of Lexington's first burial grounds. *Peter Brackney*.

Right: The final resting place of King Solomon, who "had a royal heart" and was the city's hero of the 1833 cholera epidemic. Because he drank only alcohol and no water, he did not become ill and buried many of the city's dead. *Peter Brackney*.

opening her own first brothel in 1881. Eventually, she would run the "most orderly of disorderly houses" on Megowan Street in Lexington's east end.

The tallest building in the Western Suburb is the St. Paul's Catholic Church on West Short Street; when it was completed in 1868, it was the tallest building in Lexington. It was described as a "perfect example of Gothic Revival architecture." Two doors down is Parker Place, so named because it was part of a larger tract owned by Eliza Parker (Mary Todd

Lincoln's grandmother). Captain John B. Wilgus later acquired the land and had the "largest scale and most elaborate residential building in the neighborhood" constructed. The Orphans Society of Lexington, formed in 1833 and still in existence, is the second oldest of such societies; it acquired the property and utilized it as an orphanage from 1907 until 1975.

The First Baptist Church, across Main Street from the convention center, was built in 1913 in the Collegiate Gothic Style. Three former Baptist churches occupied the site, as did Lexington's earliest burying ground. In fact, it was here that King Solomon buried the dead from the 1833 cholera epidemic. A decade and a half later, most of the bodies were relocated to the newly organized Lexington Cemetery.

WOODWARD HEIGHTS

Woodward Heights was subdivided in the late 1800s; its architecture is largely intact and of that period. The area was added to the National Register in 1980 and was made a local historic district in 1987. It was named for early developer J.C. Woodward and sits on part of a four-hundred-acre tract of land that was granted to Colonel Robert Patterson in 1776.

Between High and Maxwell Streets are two one-way streets that make up the core of this neighborhood. The northbound Merino Street is named for the soft-wooled sheep that grazed here in the early 1800s as part of a business venture to capitalize on the breed's popularity. The southbound Madison Place is named after a Lexington lawyer, Colonel Madison C. Johnson. Johnson once owed the thirty-plus acres that make up Woodward Heights, and his house, the Botherum, is the neighborhood's centerpiece.

Botherum is a U-shaped mansion that combines Grecian, Roman and Gothic elements. Within the U was an enclosed garden. Exterior walls vary from rough limestone to brick with a plaster surface to mimic stone. It is believed that M.C. Johnson worked closely with local builder-architect John McMurtry on the design. In Botherum, Johnson sought to build a temple not to himself but to his late wife. She had died twenty-three years earlier during childbirth. The story parallels that of the grief-stricken Shah Jahan, whose love for his wife, who also died in the delivery of a child, inspired the construction of the Taj Mahal in India. For that reason, Botherum has been nicknamed Lexington's Taj Mahal. The year after Johnson's death, his heirs sold Botherum and the surrounding acreage to developer J.C. Woodward, who quickly subdivided the Woodward Heights subdivision.

5

FAITH IN THE BLUEGRASS

Heaven must be a Kentucky kind of place.

It is a popular saying attributed to a minister in early Kentucky. Without a doubt, Kentucky has a rich religious history. Some scholars have suggested that Kentucky was settled with more religious fervor than any other region in the United States except Utah. Kentucky is located at the northern edge of the Bible Belt, which covers much of the southeastern United States. Over fifty religious denominations or faiths are represented in Lexington alone. It is almost impossible to count the number of churches in central Kentucky today.

Catholicism arrived in Kentucky in 1775 with the coming of a couple families to Mercer County. A decade later, a group of about 25 Catholic families from Maryland settled near Bardstown. By the time Kentucky achieved statehood seven years later, other distinct Catholic colonies had sprung up in that area. A priest was assigned to the area in 1787, and another priest followed. In 1793, the first priest ordained in the United States—Father Stephen T. Badin—came to Kentucky from Baltimore, Maryland. In 1808, Pope Pius VII established America's fourth diocese (after Boston, New York, and Baltimore) at Bardstown, Kentucky. The counties around Bardstown became known as Kentucky's "Catholic Holy Land" and remains home to the Proto-Cathedral of St. Joseph at Bardstown as well as many parishes, convents, and the Abbey of Gethsemani. In 1841, the see of the diocese was moved from Bardstown to Louisville. Kentucky's

Catholic population has been divided into four dioceses. The Diocese of Lexington, established in 1988, is the newest diocese in Kentucky.

At Cane Ridge in Bourbon County, it is estimated that some twelve thousand people gathered in August 1801 for a revival. At successive meetings, as many as thirty thousand ultimately assembled. It was the first significant church camp meeting, an American tradition of combining tents, camping, and spirituality. For decades, itinerant ministers used this pattern to convert followers. At Cane Ridge, this Great Revival sought unity. Early Kentucky settler Colonel Robert Patterson attempted to describe the scene:

> *Of all ages, from 8 years and upwards; male and female; rich and poor; the blacks; and of every denomination; those in favour of it, as well as those, at the instant in opposition to it, and railing against it, have instantaneously laid motionless on the ground. Some feel the approaching symptoms by being under deep convictions; their heart swells, their nerves relax, and in an instant they become motionless and speechless, but generally retain their senses....He went on to describe other manifestations which continued from* "one hour to 24."

Cane Ridge was part of a period of religiosity in the United States during the early nineteenth century known as the Second Great Awakening. Another movement from New York spread into Kentucky during this time. At the beginning of 1805, eleven Shaker communities existed in New York. Shakerism, properly known as the United Society of Believers in Christ's Second Appearing, was largely founded by Mother Ann Lee. Mother Ann emigrated from England, and she preached at a time when female religious leaders were quite rare. The worship style of Shakerism is noted for is "shaking" style of dancing, though the movements more orderly and symbolic than outsiders might have believed. Ultimately, the Shakers established more than twenty communities in the United States, including two in Kentucky. The community at Pleasant Hill has been restored and is a site worth visiting in Mercer County.

Presbyterians, Episcopalians, Methodists, and Baptists all found their way to Kentucky along with many other religious orders. Schools and colleges were established by various denominations to educate the population in both the liberal arts as well as in their respective faiths.

There are significant historic churches throughout the Bluegrass region. Many are architecturally unique or significant, while others may have had

Cane Ridge Meeting House in Bourbon County, Kentucky. *University of Kentucky Libraries.*

ministers or priests or parishioners who significantly contributed to their communities. Partial histories of a handful of unique Lexington churches from different traditions follow.

ST. PAUL AFRICAN METHODIST EPISCOPAL CHURCH

The African Methodist Episcopal Church has a long history in the United States. Although the denomination did not factor into the religious fabric of Lexington, Kentucky, in its earliest years, the denomination has been a vital part of the community for nearly two hundred years. No single structure embodies the A.M.E. Church in Lexington more than St. Paul's on North Upper Street.

In 1820, the Methodist Church (established in 1789) started a mission church in a stable of a member on North Upper Street. That mission on North Upper Street would become, over time, the St. Paul A.M.E. Church. This historically Black congregation meets in a building that was erected on the site of the original stable in 1826. Today, that structure is

Saint Paul's A.M.E. Church in Lexington was once a site on the Underground Railroad. *University of Kentucky Libraries.*

said to be the oldest continually used house of worship in Lexington. Over the years, it was expanded to meet the needs of the growing church body. Significant renovations and expansion projects occurred in 1850, 1877, 1906, and 1986.

African Methodist Episcopal Denomination

In 1787, a former slave by the name of Richard Allen helped establish the AME Church in Philadelphia as it split from the Methodist Episcopal Church. Six years earlier, Allen had purchased his freedom. Allen, along with the Reverend Absalom Jones, regularly worshipped at Philadelphia's St. George's ME Church.

The church had separated its African American congregants by having them seated around the room's perimeter. One Sunday in 1787, Reverend Absalom Jones, however, began his prayers prior to the service closer to the middle of the sanctuary. A sexton ordered Allen's friend to get up and told Jones that he "must not kneel here." Interrupting Jones's prayers, the sexton persisted. Jones ultimately responded to the sexton that he ought to "wait until prayer is over, and I will get up and trouble you no more."

After the conclusion of their prayers, all of the African American congregants worshipping at St. George's rose and departed the church. The moment is perceived as the beginning of the A.M.E. denomination.

Methodism in Lexington and the Beginning of St. Paul AME

In 1789, a Methodist Church was established in Lexington on the east end of town in a cabin that stood at what is today the southwest corner of East Short and Deweese Streets. It was the first Methodist church west of the Allegheny Mountains and one of the first one hundred Methodist churches in the country. In 1822, the congregation erected a new, two story church on the north side of Short Street between Limestone Street and Upper Street. Finally, in 1840, it moved to its present site on High Street between Upper and Mill Streets. The land had previously been the location of a German Lutheran church and schoolhouse that burned in 1815. The current sanctuary, built in 1907, is the second on the property. Until 1866, when its Black members left to join the congregation of St. Paul, it was a mixed-race congregation.

After the Civil War concluded, St. Paul (along with another three hundred predominately Black ME churches) withdrew from what was then known as the ME Church Conference of the South and affiliated with the A.M.E. Church. And for many years, the church continued to grow and build.

A Pillar of the Community

St. Paul's legacy extends far beyond its walls. During the era of slavery, the church functioned as a station on the Underground Railroad. Although not safely accessible today, a narrow twisting staircase behind the chancel rises to a small hidden room above the sanctuary that once served as a place of refuge for slaves on their way toward freedom.

Following the Civil War, the church hosted discussions about the education of Black Kentuckians. Members of St. Paul AME helped organize both the Colored Orphan Industrial Home and the Phyllis Wheatley YWCA. An 1885 assembly at St. Paul A.M.E. on the subject of Black education led toward the creation of what became Kentucky State University. The role that this church and its congregants played in promoting the causes of justice and equality within the commonwealth are unparalleled.

A Notable Landmark

According to Clay Lancaster, the "main fabric" of St. Paul A.M.E. "remains the oldest house of worship in Lexington." The 1827 agreement by which the congregation acquired the property noted a forty-by-sixty-five-foot brick meetinghouse on the site. Though that agreement has often been referred to as a deed, the transfer could not have fully taken place at that time because of property ownership restrictions against African American property ownership, although it may have been binding on the ME Church, South under canon law.

A remodeling in 1878 raised the roof over the narrow, hidden passageways where slaves took refuge on the Underground Railroad. And the 1906 remodeling resulted in the main entrance to the church being on the southeast corner of the sanctuary rather than through a door at the façade's midpoint. The significance of this place has earned it a designation from the city of Lexington as one of only two local historic landmarks.

CENTRAL CHRISTIAN

In 1816, a small group of Christians established a brick meetinghouse for worship under the leadership of Reverend Barton W. Stone. After worshipping in several locations, this growing congregation acquired the deed to a larger meetinghouse on Hill Street (now High Street). The Hill Street Church had been constructed as a cotton factory, and its expansion and renovation as a Christian Church were completed in 1831.

It was in this place that two early spiritual leaders on the frontier—"Raccoon" John Smith and Barton W. Stone—shook hands to lay down their differences in Christian unity. Divisions did return to the congregation, but the ranks of the congregation grew from twenty-four in 1831 to about three hundred in a decade's time. Far too large for its location, Hill Street Christian Church moved to Main Street in 1842.

In 1843, it was in this new place of worship that a great debate on Christian baptism lasted sixteen days. The debate, moderated by Henry Clay, began on November 15 and lasted to December, with debate lasting at least four hours each day except Sunday. A historic marker marks the site of the Main Street Christian Church:

> *Built on this site in 1842. The 12-day Campbell-Rice debate on Christian Baptism, etc., was held here Nov. 1843, Hon. Henry Clay presiding.*

It was in the new Main Street Christian Church building that the congregation experienced other struggles. Its pre–Civil War minister, Dr. Winthrop Hopson, resigned "because of his well-known loyalty to the South." He became the chaplain for General John Hunt Morgan. The church called John W. McGarvey as his successor. Despite the "many vicissitudes" brought by war, McGarvey's pacifist tendencies helped maintain unity among his flock (described as "an unbroken fellowship") at the church.

Becoming Central Christian Church

The Main Street Christian Church membership roster swelled to 914 by 1891. In December of that year, the site of the old Masonic Temple, at the northeast corner of Walnut and Short Streets, was acquired for $12,100 and the old temple razed. This was the site of Lexington Lodge No. 25, so numbered as the twenty-fifth lodge of freemasonry in the Commonwealth of Virginia, having been established in 1788. The lodge was renumbered Lexington Lodge No. 1 when the Grand Lodge of Kentucky was established in 1800.

The site is also, according to John D. Wright Jr., the locale of one of the most significant events between settlers and Native Americans in early Lexington history. A group of settlers was gathering logs in this vicinity when the natives began to track the settlers as they retreated toward the blockhouse. En route, John Wymore was overtaken, shot, and nearly scalped but for the efforts of other settlers who inflicted the same gruesome fate upon Wymore's assailant.

And so it was on these dark, bloody, and significant grounds that the old Masonic Temple once stood and upon which the cornerstone for a new church was laid during a service held in the evening on August 7, 1893. The cornerstone of the church itself rested on the foundation of that same Masonic Temple.

Less than a year later, a final service was held at Main Street Christian Church on July 15, 1894. The following Sunday, July 22, 1894, the main auditorium of the new church building was filled for 11:00 a.m. services, while the dedication service at 3:30 that afternoon was attended by over one thousand individuals. It was a dedication not only of the new building but also of the new name for the congregation: Central Christian Church.

The Finest Church Building in Kentucky

Journalists reporting on the dedication noted that the new Central Christian Church was considered "to be the finest church building in Kentucky and one of the finest in the nation." Under the headline "A Beautiful Edifice," those at the *Lexington Leader* wrote that "among the many magnificent buildings now in process of erection in this city, none, perhaps will be more conspicuous than the new house of worship in the Central Christian Church." From the exterior, the church is designed in the Richardsonian Romanesque style. At first glance, the ninety-five-foot gray stone tower that rises at the church's southwest corner is the most handsome feature of this house of worship, and it features accents in both brown stone and similarly colored terra cotta.

Originally, paired steps along both Walnut and Short Streets surrounded the base of this tower, with each leading toward a "triple arch of brown stone." The symmetrical entrances to the sanctuary were each below the church's primary gables, and each gable contained a "rose window thirteen feet in diameter." The inner sanctuary is octagonal in shape with significant transepts under each of the gables to effect the shape of a cruciform.

Four additional rose windows are historically iconic to the church, with each representing one of the four Gospels: Matthew, Mark, Luke, and John. At times, those visiting Central Christian are challenged to find each of the

Central Christian Church (Disciples of Christ) in Lexington. *University of Kentucky Libraries*.

four Gospel windows. But all fall short. According to church records, the window representing the Gospel of St. John "opposite the baptistery was removed or covered after a fire in the 1930s."

Tested by Fire

It was about midnight on Thursday, January 19, 1933, when fire struck Central Christian Church, causing significant fire damage to the roof and water damage to both the pews and floor. Although it was not a total loss, morning services could not be held at Central for over twenty-one months.

Other community locales like the Kentucky Theatre served as a house of worship in the interim.

During the renovation, the Moeller organ was relocated from a central location to its current location behind the baptistry. It was the same baptistry that, according to the October 21, 1902 edition of the *Lexington Herald*, "Patrolman James Dodd, while searching for a burglar, fell into."

Through the post-fire renovation, the sanctuary took a simpler appearance, particularly on and behind the chancel.

Before becoming president or even the governor of California, movie star and General Electric Theatre star Ronald Reagan came to Lexington in 1955. During his visit, he visited Central Christian Church to deliver a "witness" to the congregation. Ronald Reagan was one of three presidents to be affiliated in some capacity with the Disciples of Christ denomination.

The Municipal Building

In 1928, the City of Lexington dedicated a new city hall directly behind Central Christian Church. It fronted Walnut Street at the eastern terminus of Barr Street. At that time, a grand civic center was proposed; it could have shifted the centrality of downtown Lexington ever so slightly to the northeast. But the proposal was not to be. In the 1960s, the city demanded more space and covered the yellow brick municipal building with "a boxlike addition" that destroyed the beautiful and iconic façade. This facility would later become the home of the Fayette District Court, a purpose that became unnecessary with the completion of the dual courthouses on North Limestone in 2002, leading to Central Christian's acquisition of the property and the demolition of the much-modified municipal building.

A Kentucky Tradition

Central Christian Church is affiliated with the Disciples of Christ denomination, which was formally organized in 1968, though its historic name reaches back to the early days of Central Christian Church. At the Cane Ridge Meeting House in Bourbon County, Kentucky, a religious revival occurred in 1801. At the revival were Baptists, Methodists, and Presbyterians, among others, and many sought to do away with denominational barriers.

Arising from the revival was a new Christian church denomination espousing the authority of the Bible and claiming "no creed but Christ."

One of the earliest congregations of this religious movement, called the Restoration Movement, included those who gathered in 1816 in Lexington under the leadership of Reverend Barton Stone and would ultimately evolve into the Central Christian Church.

Central Christian's import to the Restoration Movement continued through its planting of additional churches and its role in supporting the College of the Bible (later Lexington Theological Seminary). As a result, Central is a landmark of faith not only in Lexington but also for an entire religious movement.

ST. PAUL CATHOLIC

The first Catholic church in Lexington was the Church of Saint Peter on North Limestone, built in 1837. Prior to the first Sunday of Advent in that year, Catholics in Lexington worshipped first in private homes, in a log cabin, and in a one-story brick Gothic chapel on West Third Street.

But the North Limestone church, too, was quickly outgrown, and funds were raised for the construction of a new church. In 1864, the *Lexington Transcript* reported that the Catholic congregation would "redouble their efforts in raising funds for a new church edifice, their present church being too small" and wished that the endeavor would be successful and that "a noble structure [would] soon rise up…as an ornament to our city."

Following the conclusion of the Civil War, on November 12, 1865, a processional ceremony traversing the streets of Lexington left the St. Peter Church and concluded on West Short Street, culminating in the laying of a cornerstone. Construction, though delayed for want of funds, was completed in 1868. On the occasion, the *Lexington Observer and Reporter* announced,

> *On Sunday last, that beautiful specimen of church architecture, which the Catholics of this city have erected under difficulties and in the face of obstacles that would have discouraged or have been insurmountable to a less persevering people, was consecrated to the services of religion, and henceforth, it will be known as Saint Paul Church. By the addition of this splendid edifice to our public buildings, our city has gained its brightest ornament, and the liberality, energy, and piety that saw it to its successful completion will have in it the lasting and most enduring monument.*

The old church on North Limestone remained as a mission of St. Paul's, eventually becoming in 1909 its own parish. That structure was demolished in 1930 to make way for the federal courthouse and post office on Barr Street with the new St. Peter's, also on Barr Street, being finished the year before.

The parish described the new St. Paul Church as "one of the most perfect examples of Gothic Revival architecture in the country." In 1884, Benedict Joseph Webb found the appointments of St. Paul Church "little inferior to most cathedrals." Following the Second Vatican Council, the order of worship in the Catholic Church was changed. This, coupled with a deterioration in the condition of St. Paul's "appointments," resulted in a stripping of much of the grandeur that once welcomed worshippers here.

Its spire, at 210 feet, made it for years the tallest structure in Lexington. In 1875, the Short Street entrance was improved by the addition of "broad front steps," though these stone steps were replaced with cement in 1906. And in 1883, the church acquired a clock for its tower from Howard's

The hands of the first clocktower in Lexington during renovation. St. Paul's Catholic Church was the city's tallest building when completed. *Peter Brackney*.

Clockworks in Boston, Massachusetts, for $1,600. The *Lexington Transcript* described this "valuable improvement" and found that "the new clock in the tower of St. Paul church is now in perfect running order." It was the only church tower in Lexington with a clock.

According to Clay Lancaster, construction of the building "has been claimed for both Cincinnatus Shryock and Julian S. Hogland, both of Lexington," while the design was of Messrs. Pickett & Son of Cincinnati, Ohio.

Catholicism in Lexington

Catholicism in Lexington dates to 1794, though Catholic families certainly were present before that date. In 1787, a missionary was sent to the region, but the Catholics of Fayette County were organized under Father Stephen T. Badin, who arrived in January 1794.

In 1791, Badin escaped his native France as the revolutionary government persecuted Catholics there. He joined Benedict Joseph Flaget on his journey to the New World; Flaget would later become the bishop of Bardstown upon its creation.

Left: Father Bekkers, the first priest of St. Paul's, is buried under this stone in the church narthex. *Peter Brackney*.

Right: Father Stephen Badin. *National Library and Archives of Quebec*.

Badin continued his theological studies in Baltimore, Maryland, where he, on May 25, 1793, became the first priest ordained in the United States. Bishop Carroll of Baltimore sent Father Badin to Lexington, where he served until about 1820, when he returned to France. Father Badin later returned to the United States and labored for the Church in the Great Lakes region. Land he acquired, and later donated back to the church, would become the site of Notre Dame University.

Father Bekkers

The first pastor of St. Paul Catholic Church was Father John H. Bekkers. Father Bekkers helped to strengthen and expand the parish from his arrival in 1864. During his pastorate, St. Paul's acquired a rectory as well as grounds for a parochial school. Father Bekkers also helped to establish a Catholic hospital in the city. In the words of Benedict Joseph Webb, as written in his *Centenary on Catholicism in Kentucky*,

> *The mere mention of the results of his labors as these affected the material interests of his parish will sufficiently indicate the measure of his capabilities. But still more wonderful were his labors and their fruits in giving heavenward direction to the minds and hearts, the aspirations and the hopes of those to whom he had been sent of God that he might lead them aright in the paths of virtue and religion.*

In addition, Father Bekkers was instrumental in the church's acquisition of land for the Calvary Cemetery on the south side of Leestown Road across from the Lexington Cemetery. Father Bekkers died in 1878 and, per his wishes, is buried beneath a marble slab in the narthex of the church. The marble slab bears an inscription:

> *In Memory of JOHN H BEKKERS, born at Druten Holland April 22, 1821; Ordained a Priest, 1844; Came to America, 1853; To Lexington, 1864; Founded this Church, November 12, 1865; Dedicated October 18, 1868 Remained its Pastor until he died, September 12, 1878; His remains lie in the vault beneath. R.I.P.*

Parsonage and School

On one side of St. Paul Catholic Church is its parsonage and on the other is its school. The original rectory acquired by Father Bekkers was demolished in 1886, and a new parsonage was ready for occupancy the following year. The earlier structure, an old but substantial dwelling, had been the residence of Robert S. Todd and the birthplace of his daughter, Mary Todd, who would later marry Abraham Lincoln and become first lady of the United States.

Upon the old parsonage's demolition, the bricks were used in the construction of the new parsonage, and many of the building materials were also incorporated into the gatehouse at Calvary Cemetery.

On the other side of the church stands the old St. Paul school, which closed in 1988 due to low attendance. The building later reopened as part of the regional Sts. Peter & Paul School. The present parochial school on West Short Street was constructed in 1913, though a Catholic education could be had on this site since 1867. The Sisters of Charity of Nazarene took over the school in 1887 and renamed it to correspond with the adjacent parish. In 1900, the school became coeducational.

The school's design features seven bays atop a high foundation. According to Sanborn Maps, the earlier pre-1913 schools on the site were closer to the street. This would have caused the approach along Short Street from the east to conceal from view the church until you were upon it, while the 1913 structure includes a lawn that reveals the grandeur of the church itself.

FIRST AFRICAN BAPTIST

Elijah Warner purchased the former Methodist Meeting House (1822) on Short Street in 1823. Warner, a clockmaker and cabinetmaker, was born in 1787 in Massachusetts and came to Kentucky in 1810. Warner became a slaveholder, and one of his slaves was Elijah Hayden. Warner purchased Hayden from Reverend Adam Rankin, the noted Presbyterian minister, in exchange for two carriage horses. Years later, Warner sold Hayden's wife and son to another slaveholder, who subsequently sold Hayden's family. Tragically, Hayden would never see his family again.

Ultimately, Hayden, too, would be sold by Elijah Warner. Hayden remarried and ultimately escaped the trials of slavery by following the north star of freedom along the Underground Railroad to Boston,

First African Baptist Church was established and built by Lexington's slaves and freed Black population on East Short Street. They began worshipping in 1790, and the present structure was built in 1850. *Peter Brackney*.

Massachusetts. There, he became quite involved in both abolitionist and Republican politics. He was elected once to the Massachusetts state legislature, and his home near Beacon Hill served as a boardinghouse along the Underground Railroad.

Hayden rose out of slavery to a most significant position. The space where he once tirelessly labored, too, became a significant Lexington landmark. Upon Elijah Warner's death in 1829, the property at the southwest corner of Short and Deweese Streets was willed to his half brother, Alfred. Just four years later, Alfred sold the property to the First African Baptist Church. The congregation would remain at this location for the next 131 years.

The location at Short and Deweese was not the congregation's first. Around 1790, First African began meeting in a cabin located on land owned by one of Lexington's founders, John Maxwell. Maxwell afforded the land to the Black worshippers and assisted in the cabin's construction, which could have been found in the proximity of what is today the intersection of Avenue of Champions and Lexington Avenue.

Two additional locations—both on Mulberry (Limestone) Street—filled the gap between the church's cabin and its long-standing home on East Short Street. It was also during the time of these intermediary locations that the congregation divided, the separatists becoming what is today the Historic Pleasant Green Missionary Baptist Church on Maxwell Street.

The Old Captain

The history of First African Baptist cannot be told without turning first to the Upper Spotsylvania Baptist Church in Virginia, located between the James and Rappahannock Rivers. There, in 1767, a Baptist church was founded by Lewis Craig; Craig's ordination followed in 1770. Here, the Baptists worshipped until 1781, when they departed "lock, stock, and Bible" for Kentucky as what has become known as the Traveling Church.

George W. Ranck wrote an account of this Traveling Church in 1891 that included the following:

> *The modern exodus was no small affair for its day and generation. The moving train included with church members, their children, Negro slaves and other emigrants (who, for better protection, had attached themselves to an organized expedition), between five and six hundred souls. It was the largest body of Virginians that ever set out for Kentucky at one time. And not only the members but nearly everything else pertaining to Craigs Church was going. Its official books and records, its simple communion service, the treasured old Bible from the pulpit—nearly everything in fact but the building itself was moving away together.*

Ranck's account went on to describe the roles taken by the slaves during the exodus: toting household possessions, clearing "obstructions from the miserable road," and leading the well-packed animals that carried the bulk of that which was being transported. Among these were Peter Durrett and his wife, who were enslaved by Lewis Craig's brother, Joseph. Joseph Craig had owned only Peter's wife immediately prior to the exodus but had traded another slave for Peter in part so that husband and wife would remain together.

Although the sentimental argument for why Joseph Craig traded another slave for Durrett likely has merit, the trade had a practical reason as well. In 1779, Durrett had been brought to the Bluegrass by Colonel

James Estill during his expedition of the area, so Durrett had familiarity with the region and could serve as a guide for the Traveling Church. As a baptized Christian and member of the Craig family's household, he, too, was involved in ministry.

Once the Craigs and the Traveling Church temporarily settled at the head of Boone Creek, Ranck wrote that the Durretts "hired themselves of their master." This meant that although their ownership did not change, they were free to live apart from their master but that their earned wages were to be remitted to him. It was at this time that Peter Durrett came to Lexington, where they continued their ministry from John Maxwell's farm.

In addition to the church established on Maxwell's farm, a religious training school for African Americans was begun on Maxwell's farm in 1816. Levi Todd, another Lexington pioneer and the grandfather of Mary Todd Lincoln, helped finance this endeavor. By 1820, twenty-two African Americans were recommended by Durrett to become Baptist ministers to spread the good news among Kentucky's Black population.

Although Peter Durrett died in 1823, his ministry to the free and enslaved Black communities of Lexington reached hundreds, and the church he began, which eventually became the First African Baptist Church, was the first independent Black church west of the Alleghenies.

The Growth of First African

Like Durrett, London Ferrill was born in Virginia. A gifted preacher, he was ordained in 1821 and became the minister at First African Baptist Church after Durrett's death. The ministerial styles and the way in which they involved themselves in the larger community were quite different: Durrett remained enslaved until his death and was never an ordained minister (though that was not an impediment in the Separate Baptist tradition).

Ferrill, on the other hand, received his freedom in 1820 after he was called into the ministry; his former owners freed him so that he could be free to preach the Gospel to whomever he could. He was a Regular Baptist who brought First African into the Elkhorn Baptist Association. And his friendships and circle of influence included some of Lexington's elite White families. There are some accounts of Ferrell preaching to White congregations soon after his arrival in Kentucky, another opportunity that distinguishes him from Peter Durrett.

London Ferrill's assumption of the First African pulpit created an opportunity for the church to grow both in stature and in number. And grow it did. But it would be disingenuous to not acknowledge the strife the faithful from Durrett's church faced with the new minister and his different approach; like in so many churches, change brought about a degree of division. Even so, the First African Baptist Church grew in number to as many as 1,820. It was reported to be the largest congregation in Kentucky at the time—Black or White. And over 5,000 souls were baptized during Ferrill's ministry at the church.

London Ferrill died on October 12, 1854. He is buried in the Episcopal Cemetery on Third Street—one of only a few African Americans to be interred there. His legacy in the community was enhanced by his role during the cholera epidemics of the 1830s. During these reigns of illness—in which nearly a tenth of Lexington's population died—only London Ferrill was willing to offer the dead a "good Christian burial." His own funeral, however, drew an estimated five thousand mourners in one of the largest funerals in Lexington history.

A New First African

It was also during the pastorate of London Ferrill that ground was broken on the church building at Short and Deweese Streets on a portion of the foundation that had previously served as the Methodist Church. Although construction began around 1850, it was not completed until nearly two years after Ferrill's death.

The new structure has been described in its National Register of Historic Places registration as an "example of a mid-nineteenth century Italianate style Protestant chapel." And in simple verse, another described the First African Baptist Church simply as striking by noting its soaring arched windows and the elegance of its columned portico, coupled with its impressive mass.

Those columns were an addition in the 1920s, along with an attached annex that is decidedly Tudor in style. The same year that the cornerstone for the annex was laid, 1926, another minister took the pulpit at First African Baptist: Homer Nutter. Reverend Nutter ministered here for almost five decades, during which the church became a force in the local civil rights movement.

FIRST PRESBYTERIAN

The Mount Zion Presbyterian Church, Lexington's earliest Presbyterian congregation, was established around 1784. It is likely that the congregation would have in its earliest days met in a log meetinghouse, which the congregants sought to expand as early as 1788. Mount Zion is a reference to the location at the heart of a 190-acre tract near where the University of Kentucky's Agriculture Experimental Station now stands.

A second story about the birthplace of the Presbyterian Church in Lexington is contained in George W. Ranck's 1884 *Guide to Lexington, Kentucky*:

> *Colonel Robert Patterson, the founder of Lexington, was a member of this congregation, which first worshipped in a rude log cabin, on the southeastern corner of Walnut and Short, and he and other members frequently attended services with rifles in their hands, for the Christian pioneer…had to literally "watch" (for Indians) as well as "pray."*

Under then-Virginia law, an unauthorized (non-Anglican/Episcopalian) church could not be located within the bounds of a county seat. Thus, Lexington, as the seat of Fayette County, could have no house of worship within its limits excepting that of the Anglican persuasion, in Lexington's case, a Methodist church. It was a law not retained by the Kentuckians when they achieved statehood in 1792.

Notices contained in the *Kentucky Gazette* sought the "payment of subscriptions in bacon, hemp, linen, wheat, or corn." The Mount Zion congregants diverged into two groups, with the majority locating to land acquired from the Lexington trustees on a portion of the public square fronting Mill Street. It was here that a meetinghouse was constructed. The satisfaction with being in the heart of the city was short-lived; its noisy location soon prompted the church to reconsider its downtown locale. In 1808, the site was abandoned in favor of a new one-and-one-half-story brick church at Broadway and Second Streets.

It was in this building that, in July 1817, lightning struck the church's cupola, resulting in the electrocution of two women in the pews during Wednesday evening services. According to an account reported in the *Western (KY) Monitor*, the balance of the Presbyterian congregation hung their heads in awe of the God "who holds the lightnings [*sic*] in his hand, and directs them where to strike." Meanwhile, it was further reported that the lightning strike caused a woman to regain her hearing in one ear—it had been lost for three decades.

In these days, pew rentals were used to raise funds for the church. In November 1822, the *Kentucky Reporter* included a report that "First Presbyterian has pews to rent and application can be made to the treasurer." But by 1846, the *Observer & Reporter* noted the change in policy: the church membership "voted to have all pews free hereafter." The change did not last; pew rentals returned to First Presbyterian in July 1857.

The same year, the congregation sought a new house of worship, even going so far as to consult with architect Benjamin Latrobe. Latrobe's plans, however, never materialized. Instead, a two-story brick church was built on the same location in 1857. This building has been described as "Gothic in form, Grecian in detail, and Romanesque in fenestration." Thirteen years after the church's completion, the Presbyterians sold the building to the trustees of the Main Street Christian Church, which would house a second congregation in this space. That second congregation became independent of the Main Street Christian Church to become Broadway Christian Church; it remained in the sanctuary and stills worships at the location today.

Returning to Mill Street

With the sale of the church building at Second and Broadway, the congregants of First Presbyterian Church had plans laid for their return to Mill Street. Their new sanctuary, however, would not be completed until 1872. During the interim period, the congregants of the Presbyterian Church used temporary worship space at the Melodeon Hall on Main Street. The *Lexington Observer and Reporter* reported the same on April 30, 1870: "First Presbyterian Church now worshipping in Melodeon Hall and for some months to come."

Worship occurred on the upper floor of the Melodeon Hall, a structure that is still standing at the southwest corner of Main and Upper Streets opposite the courthouse. The Melodeon Hall was built in 1849 to replace an earlier two-story brick structure, but its façade was significantly modified in 1858 with the handsome addition of cast iron. A drugstore operated in the predecessor building from 1817 until its demolition and in the first floor of the Melodeon Hall until 1993. As a result, the Melodeon Hall is often referred to as the McAdams and Morford Building, the name of this long-standing tenant.

While the Presbyterians worshipped behind the cast-iron façade of the Melodeon Hall, work was underway on their new house of worship. On May 8, 1872, the *Lexington Observer and Reporter* offered its readers a detailed sketch of the new church. It is believed that the architect, Cincinnatus Shryock, wrote the description:

> *It is a plain Gothic Structure, built of brick neatly oiled and penciled. The doors and windows of the façade and tower have cut stone hood mouldings, and the buttresses cut stone sloping copings. The front gables are also covered with cut stone copings supported by cut stone and brick corbels. Further than this no attempt was made at external decoration....From the lobby three doors open into the audience room, and a flight of stairs on each side of the tower leads to the gallery....The ceiling is 31 feet high from the floor and is grained; the main vault being a semi-ellipse intersected by gothic vaults over the windows and recesses in front and rear....The windows, on account of their proportions and beautiful stained glass, form a very attractive feature of the audience room. All of the wood work of this room including the wainscoting, pews, pulpit, pulpit steps, and gallery front, is of oak, ash, and walnut in varnish, and is arranged to produce a very pleasing effect.*

The most prominent feature of the church, however, is its 18-foot-square, 180-foot tower, and spire at the symmetrical center of the Mill Street façade. The tower, through which thirteen steps ascend to the lobby mentioned above, is 18 feet square and rises 100 feet before the spire rises the final 80 feet toward the heavens.

When first completed, the depth of the audience room was fifty-four feet, five inches long, but the chancel was extended sixteen additional feet toward Market Street during a remodeling in 1897. The congregation had contemplated a new church altogether, but the decision was made to renovate and not replace the then just twenty-five-year-old church. The remodeling and expansion included the addition of a fifth bay to the length of the building, and it also resulted in the addition of a Kimball organ, the pipes of which were originally hand stenciled. This stenciling was rediscovered during an extensive cleaning to the organ in the early 2010s, and the stenciled design has been reincorporated onto the mighty pipes.

4 Congregations; 2 Churches; 1 Civil War

Reverend Robert J. Breckinridge served First Presbyterian from 1847 to 1853, the era when the church met in a building at the corner of North Broadway and Second Streets. Nicknamed the "Napoleon of the Pulpit," Breckinridge favored the gradual emancipation of slaves, though he vehemently denied being an abolitionist. For the era, this was a practical solution. As described in the church's own history, "Pastors who opposed [slavery] risked splitting their congregations or inviting attacks on their property, family, or persons." At the time, Lexington was central to the slave trade, and the local economy was built on the institution.

The politics of Kentucky pervaded the congregation of First Presbyterian during the Civil War. With many slaveholders counted on the congregation's membership rolls, slavery was largely accepted. But secession from the United States was not. The Second Presbyterian Church members maintained similar views in their own congregation.

But as the Civil War continued, Lexington found itself continually torn by the presence of, at different times, both Union and Confederate forces. The suspension of habeas corpus and the emancipation of slaves added tension to the political climate. Divisions within the community and the churches grew. By the end of the war, a split could no longer be avoided.

In 1866, the Presbytery of West Lexington was divided along political lines, creating a Northern Presbyterian Church and a Southern Presbyterian Church. Both First and Second Presbyterian divided along these lines, with each group hiring its own minister. Thus, First Presbyterian had two congregations, each with its own minister: one aligned with the success of the Union and the other sympathetic to the Lost Cause.

In 1869, a practical solution developed, realigning the memberships between the two Presbyterian churches. Those in agreement with the Southern Presbyterian Church remained at First Presbyterian, while those aligned with the Northern Presbyterian Church took attendance at Second Presbyterian. These kinds of divisions would remain part of the Presbyterian Church both in Lexington and nationally until well into the twentieth century.

Lexington's First Presbyterian Church is among those that could claim the mantle of "Lexington's church." Here, the people of this city have celebrated and mourned over the years. The funerals of senators and mayors have been held in this hallowed space, as have countless weddings and commencement ceremonies.

CHRIST CHURCH EPISCOPAL

At the northeast corner of Market and Church Streets stands the Christ Church Episcopal Church. The building sits on the same site where, in 1796, the first Episcopal Church west of the Allegheny Mountains began holding services in a "dilapidated log house," according to the church's nomination form to the National Register of Historic Places.

A week before Christmas 1845, Thomas Lewinski began to sketch his design. According to the architect's accounts, final arrangements "with Episcopal Church Committee for design and specification" were made on September 2, 1846. John McMurtry was awarded the contract to build Lewinski's design, and the project was completed in May 1848. It is believed that the architect penned this description of the new Christ Church, published the same month in the *Lexington Observer and Reporter*:

> *The new Church just finished for the use of the Episcopal Parish, in this city, as a cost, including the organ, bell and lamps, of $20,000 is one of the most chaste, beautiful and perfect specimens of the plain Gothic, which has been erected in the Western country, and reflects great credit alike upon the liberality of the Congregation, the skill in art of the Architect and Contractor, and the exquisite taste and indefatigable attention of the building committee. For a building in brick, it is one of the most massive and substantial built in modern times. The proportions though not large, are remarkably just.*

The new Christ Church would be the fourth Episcopal house of worship on the site. The land was donated in 1808 to the church by Lord William Morton and Dr. Walter Warfield. The community replaced the "dilapidated log house" with a "little brick church" in 1803, according to Clay Lancaster in his *Vestiges of the Venerable City*.

An Anglican Tradition

The Episcopal Church began as an Americanized copy of the Anglican Church, born out of the American Revolution; independence was sought in both the state and the church. Even so, the ties between the two churches on either side of the Atlantic were unmistakable.

Before the war, the first sermon preached in Kentucky was made by Reverend John Lythe at Boonesborough in 1775. Despite this factoid, the Episcopal Church was not poised to take great strides on the early frontier. In *A History of Kentucky*, Dr. Thomas D. Clark summed up the challenges for growth of the Episcopalian faith on the frontier this way: "This tells its own

Christ Church Cathedral is an Episcopal church where Henry Clay worshipped. *University of Kentucky Libraries.*

story; westerners, for the most part, detested the English social and political systems which the Episcopal Church represented. It was partly this system of society which drove the Kentucky settlers out of the eastern seaboard colonies into the West." It did, however, grow and flourish over time.

Though significant leaders and prominent citizens accepted the Episcopal faith, the organization of the Episcopal Church at Lexington was not complete until 1796. James Moore, having arrived as a teacher at the Transylvania Seminary in 1792, went back to Virginia for ordination and returned to Lexington as the Episcopal Church's first minister. When the Transylvania Seminary and the Kentucky Academy merged in 1799, Reverend Moore became the first president of the newly formed Transylvania University.

Ultimately, however, Reverend Moore, would resign his academic position so that he could give his full attention to growing the Episcopal Church. He would remain active until 1812, when health forced his retirement.

In 1809, the *Kentucky Gazette* promoted the "Scheme of a Lottery" by which the Episcopal Church sought "to raise the sum of 750 dollars, for the purpose of finishing the Episcopal church in Lexington, and toward the purchase of an organ."

Matthias Shryock and Michael Gough served as the builders for the third Episcopal Church on the site: it was "of brick covered with stucco to resemble stone, and it measured 60-by-80 feet and had an 85-foot steeple. The auditorium had a seating capacity of 800 persons, and its pews were sold to defray building expenses," all according to Clay Lancaster's description. This third structure dates to 1814.

Almost immediately, the structure was viewed by many as being obsolete and unsafe, though it would survive until the present building was completed in 1848.

A Dominating Presence

The edifice of Christ Church is a dominating presence on its corner at Market and Church Streets. Measuring fifty-nine feet by ninety-four feet, the interior ceiling bears a crucifix of intersecting arches. Its ninety-five-foot-tall square tower is described in the *Lexington Observer and Reporter* as "almost perfect of its kind." The article continues to describe the tower, the surrounding buttresses, and the ornamental cast-iron finials all of "excellent design and finish." Plaques high along the Market Street façade contain readings from Scripture that direct the purpose of the building:

In the name of the Father, and of the Son, and of the Holy Ghost. Erected Anno Domini MDCCCXLVII (1847)

God is a Spirit, and they that worship Him must worship Him in Spirit and in Truth. St. John IV.24.

Along Market Street, six bays bear a modification to the church's original five-bay-deep design. The additional sixth bay was added about a decade after the church was completed to add the space now utilized for the chancel and organ space. The addition, which took about a decade to complete, was the idea of Reverend James Morrison and became known as "Morrison's Folly." Because of mistakes by the hired architect and dissatisfaction with the project, the church terminated its contract with the architect and convinced Thomas Lewinski (the architect of the original church) to abandon his retirement and complete the addition.

Worshipped Here

Although the Episcopal Church was not immediately deemed acceptable on the frontier, many of the most prominent citizens in the Athens of the West worshipped at Christ Church. A historic marker in front of Christ Church Cathedral recognizes some of the early parishioners:

Henry Clay, statesman and orator, known as "The Great Compromiser"; John Bradford, editor of the first newspaper in Kentucky; John Wesley Hunt, merchant and financier; John Hunt Morgan, "Thunderbolt of the Confederacy"; Laura Clay, women's rights advocate. All worshipped at and contributed to the growth of Christ Church.

Each of these individuals was, at some point, a resident or visitor to Gratz Park. Henry Clay's pew is today marked with a bronze tablet. John Bradford's house was once located at the southwest corner of Second and Mill Streets; Bradford acquired the home from Thomas Hart, who was the father of Lucretia Hart, the wife of Henry Clay. It was in this home where Lucretia and Henry were wed, and it was later the home of Laura Clay (the daughter of Cassius Clay and Henry Clay's second cousin) until her death. And although the Hart-Bradford House was demolished in 1955, the home of John Wesley Hunt, Hopemont, stands across Second Street.

John Wesley Hunt was the first millionaire to make his fortune on this side of the Allegheny Mountains, deriving his wealth from various industries but primarily the growing and processing of hemp. Hunt's daughter, Henrietta, was the mother of Confederate general John Hunt Morgan.

Some of the most significant names in Lexington's history are intimately tied to Christ Church, and Christ Church is intimately tied to the history of Lexington.

TWO HISTORIC JEWISH CONGREGATIONS

Ohavay Zion

Lexington's first Jewish synagogue opened in 1914 in a former mission of First Presbyterian Church. The building that originally served the Ohavay Zion congregation remains standing at the corner of West Maxwell and Jersey Streets as the Joe Bologna's restaurant.

Prior to moving into the Maxwell Street location, the faithful of Ohavay Zion worshipped wherever space could be found, typically in stores and in the ballrooms of hotels or fraternal lodges for High Holy Days. At the dawn of the twentieth century, Lexington's orthodox Jewish community consisted of fewer than a dozen families. When merchant Joe Rosenberg learned of the availability of what would become the home of the congregation, they moved quickly to purchase and renovate the building into a fitting worship space for their services.

David Ades and his family, along with the Rosenbergs, were founding members of Ohavay Zion. Ades' dry goods building, now the home of Portofino's Restaurant on East Main Street, was built in the Chicago School style as a five-story, five-bay commercial building. The family operated here from the building's construction in 1910 until the family closed the business in 1977. David Ades emigrated to the United States from modern-day Lithuania, joining his brother in the dry goods business. His business success was shared with his community: Ades was quite involved with the Masons, the Odd Fellows, and the Elks lodges in addition to serving on Lexington's planning commission and ultimately as a city commissioner.

In 1919, Jacob Lowenthal arrived in Lexington and served as the first full-time rabbi. Over time, the congregation acquired a neighboring building, which was used for Hebrew school and social functions of the church. In 1987, the Torahs were removed from the ark and processed to a new home.

Former Main Street home of David Ades' dry goods company. *Peter Brackney*.

Temple Adath Israel

While Ohavay Zion holds the title as the oldest Jewish congregation in Lexington, the oldest continuously operating Jewish house of worship is Temple Adath Israel on North Ashland Avenue. Temple Adath Israel was formally established in 1904. Its charter read that Temple Adath Israel was established "for the purpose of religious services, a Sabbath school and other matters pertaining to the moral elevation among the Jewish people of Lexington and central Kentucky."

Before being chartered, the congregation met in 1903 at a "rented lodge hall on Short Street in downtown Lexington, where a dozen of the most prominent Jewish residents met to hold services, listen to the lecture of a visiting rabbi, and set in motion the establishment of a new congregation" according to the book *The Synagogues of Kentucky*.

In 1904, the congregation constructed and began worshipping in a synagogue on Maryland Avenue. It was the first physical synagogue in Lexington. Although still standing, the Maryland Avenue structure that

The interior of Temple Adath Israel, which is Lexington's oldest synagogue. It opened in 1926 from its prior location on Maryland Avenue. *Peter Brackney.*

once housed the synagogue had little exterior indication of function. Only a wooden sign near its door evidenced that the building was a Jewish house of worship. When the congregation moved to Ashland Avenue in 1926, the sign was brought as well.

Inside the current synagogue is a museum of both local and international Jewish history. Significantly, the temple acquired in 1987 a Torah from Turnov in what is now the Czech Republic. The Turnov Torah survived the Holocaust, and the congregation notes that it gives a "commonality with those who perished in the Holocaust," linking those souls from the past.

BEYOND DOWNTOWN

Beyond downtown Lexington and outside of Fayette County are many other historically important churches. Walnut Hill Church in Fayette County operates ecumenically but is the oldest standing Presbyterian church in Kentucky. It is situated on land donated by General Levi Todd, Mary Todd

The Old Stone Meeting House where Daniel Boone and his family were believed to have worshipped. Today, it is the home of Providence Baptist Church. *Peter Brackney*.

Lincoln's grandfather. Eighty-five individuals are interred at the historic cemetery at Walnut Hill Church.

In Clark County, the Old Stone Meeting House is the oldest Baptist church in Kentucky. It is believed that Daniel Boone and his family attended services here. Today, Providence Baptist Church holds services here. Providence has hosted services here since 1790, when it was named Providence. William Bush, a member of Boone's second Kentucky expedition, led the construction of the house of worship. A nearby historic marker indicates that the church "passed to Negro Baptists" in 1870.

Some historic churches have fallen into disrepair, while others (like Walnut Hill Church mentioned above) have been salvaged and thrive today. Some, like the former home to Ohavay Zion on Maxwell Street, have been adapted to another use.

6
AROUND THE BLUEGRASS

SPOKES ON A WHEEL

In 1609, King James of England granted the Second Charter of Virginia, which extended the boundaries of the Virginia Company two hundred miles from the Atlantic coastline. This grant included lands that had never been surveyed or even seen by Europeans. As more settlers came to the American continent and traveled westward, the Virginia colony was divided into several counties. From 1772 to 1776, Kentucky was included in what was considered Fincastle County, Virginia. Fincastle County existed only until the end of 1776, when it was subdivided into three separate counties: Washington County (now exclusively a part of Virginia), Montgomery County (which included parts of present-day Virginia and West Virginia), and Kentucky County.

Then, in 1780, Kentucky County was further divided into three counties: Jefferson, Fayette, and Lincoln. With the exception of lands in far western Kentucky, today's Kentucky borders fit entirely within this subdivision. The borders of Fayette County roughly included all lands in present-day Kentucky north of the Kentucky River. Over the next dozen years, the number of Virginia counties in the "Kentucky District" would rise to nine. And on June 1, 1792, those nine counties separated from Virginia to form the Commonwealth of Kentucky.

Today, Kentucky has 120 counties. Each is unique and different, and often a healthy competition exists among folks from neighboring counties. These rivalries are often enhanced through high school athletics. Many counties, however, arose from the desire for local governance and justice. Kentucky separated itself from Virginia because the distance to the capitol in Richmond was too far; in the same vein, Kentucky counties separated from one another so that it would be both safe and easy to obtain justice.

The eleven central Kentucky counties that surround Lexington are part of the inner Bluegrass region. In 2006, the World Monuments Fund put the Inner Bluegrass Region on its watch list as one of the world's most endangered places that was "worthy of conservation." According to that listing, the Inner Bluegrass Region is renowned for both its natural resources as well as its "more than 220 years of history and development based largely on an agrarian economy." The Inner Bluegrass Region is the birthplace of bourbon and was instrumental in the burley tobacco trade. The structures and identity of these two industries are evident across the region, as are the identities of other industries, social hierarchies, and transportation methods that made the industries so successful.

Lexington is, and always has been, the heart of the Bluegrass. In Bennett Young's 1898 *History of Jessamine County*, he described Lexington as the "political, intellectual, and commercial metropolis of Kentucky, and [it] necessarily dwarfed the surrounding towns and attracted the best trade from the counties within a radius of fifty miles." When Jessamine County was formed in 1798, just six years into Kentucky's statehood, Lexington had a population of approximately two thousand. Cincinnati, Ohio, which has since grown much larger, then had a population of only five hundred. Lexington was truly the Athens of the West, and each of the small communities surrounding it benefited from its size and culture.

Although each of Kentucky's 120 counties has a rich and unique history, each cannot be covered in this book. The Inner Bluegrass Region is a starting point but stretches from Lexington in a more northeasterly direction. Some of the region's most important historical sites, however, are to the south and west of Lexington. As you consider a visit to Lexington, it is wise to go beyond Fayette County to visit another more rural space. And take a back road to get there. In doing so, you'll get to appreciate the beauty of the region described by the World Monuments Fund as "one of America's most distinctive landscapes."

To access these different communities, one might take any of the spokes leading away from downtown Lexington. The highways were constructed to connect Lexington to other municipalities in Kentucky. This method of naming roads is not uncommon or unique to the region, though Lexington has uniquely grown as a wheel around the various spokes.

The following sections highlight each of the Kentucky counties that touches Fayette, as well as three additional counties: Boyle, Mercer, and Franklin. Clockwise from the north...

SCOTT COUNTY

Scott County is the most rapidly growing Kentucky county in terms of population—over 18.5 percent in the 2010s. A major contributor to this growth is that Georgetown, the seat of Scott County, is the home to Toyota Motor Manufacturing. The Japanese automaker broke ground on its first automobile plant in the United States in 1986. In 1989, the first American-made Toyota Camry came off the assembly line. Today, the Toyota plant manufactures the Toyota Camry, Toyota Avalon, and the Lexus ES 350. In her remarks at the groundbreaking, Kentucky's then-governor Martha Layne Collins remarked that the event showed "a growing friendship and partnership between the people of Kentucky and Toyota and between them and the people of Japan."

That friendship remains highly visible at Georgetown's YUKO-EN ON THE ELKHORN, which is the official Kentucky-Japan Friendship Garden. The six-acre garden is located along the banks of the North Elkhorn Creek. It opened in 1990 and features native plants as well as Japanese garden principles.

White explorers first came to what would become Scott County as early as 1774, when the Royal Spring was found, offering a consistent source of water. The following year, John McClelland and others built a fort overlooking the spring. McClelland's Fort, however, was abandoned the following year. In 1784, Virginia incorporated the town of Lebanon at the site at the behest of Reverend Elijah Craig. Six years later, Lebanon was renamed "George Town" after President George Washington. ROYAL SPRING PARK in downtown Georgetown encompasses the spring, which is considered to be where Craig first distilled the brown spirit, bourbon. The Royal Spring flows into the North Elkhorn Creek with waters then entering the Kentucky River.

Reverend Craig, the father of bourbon, was also involved in a host of other firsts in the county. Importantly for the future of Georgetown, Craig started the first school here with courses in the languages and sciences; the school was a forbearer of GEORGETOWN COLLEGE. Officially chartered in 1829, Georgetown College was the first Baptist college west of the Allegheny Mountains. In the wake of the Cane Ridge Revival in Bourbon County, many churches associated with the Baptist tradition left. It was intended that by organizing a college at Georgetown, the Baptists would

A foot bridge at the official Japanese American Friendship Garden, Yuko-En on the Elkhorn, in Scott County. *Peter Brackney.*

continue to maintain their influence. One of the most iconic buildings at the college is Giddings Hall. Constructed in 1840, it was named for Reverend Rockwood Giddings, who was the school's third president. It is rumored that there is a quart of bourbon under each of the columns of Giddings Hall's portico.

Another school in Scott County with historical importance is the Choctaw Indian Academy, which operated from 1825 through 1843. A historic marker on US-460 between Georgetown and Frankfort identifies the general location of the school. (It is on private land and not open to the public.) Choctaw Indian Academy was opened on the farm of Richard Mentor Johnson about five miles west of Georgetown. Richard Johnson later served as vice president during the administration of Martin Van Buren. During the twenty-three years the school operated, over six hundred students from seventeen different Native American tribes were educated here. The attempt to "civilize" and "assimilate" Native Americans at the school came at a unique time in America's history. Indian attacks, like those at the county's McClelland's Fort, caused many White settlements to be abandoned. The

Indian Removal Act of 1830, signed into law by Andrew Johnson, relocated Native Americans to reservations in often inhumane ways. The school offered, at the time, a much different model. Even as Native Americans were relocated to the Indian Territory, tribes continued to send some of their young men to the Choctaw Indian Academy in Scott County as a means for opportunity. Many alumni of the school became strong advocates for their people and leaders in their communities. One original building, likely a dormitory, from the school still stands, and there are plans for its restoration.

In addition to being vice president, Richard M. Johnson served in both houses of Congress and was a hero of the War of 1812. He and Julia Chinn, his mulatto slave, engaged in a twenty-year relationship that produced two daughters. It is rumored that, although such a marriage would have then been illegal, Richard and Julia were married in secret. Unlike many master-slave conjugal relations, this relationship appeared different. When in Washington, Richard left control of his farm, the school, and his other slaves to Julia. Julia hosted a dinner honoring Marquis de Lafayette at the family's farm in 1825; their daughter, Adaline, is reputed to have played the piano for the famous Frenchman as well.

Richard M. Johnson's parents came from Orange County, Virginia; Johnson's mother, Jemima, was the heroine at the Battle of Bryan Station in Fayette County. Johnson's sister, Sallie, married Colonel William Ward. Junius Ward was a product of that union. Junius and his wife, Matilda Viley Ward, constructed WARD HALL beginning in 1853 on land acquired by his grandfather in the 1700s. Clay Lancaster, an authority on Kentucky architecture, described the house as "largest Greek Revival house in Kentucky." Ward Hall, with more than twelve thousand square feet across four stories, was built with the tremendous wealth of the Johnson family as well as the successful Thoroughbred breeding and racing Viley family through which Junius Ward gained more than a foothold in the industry.

For a short season, Junius Ward was part of a small syndicate that owned the horse Lexington—a legendary thoroughbred who was the leading North American sire sixteen times between 1861 and 1878. Following the Civil War, Ward suffered from financial ruin and declared bankruptcy. All of his Scott County holdings, including Ward Hall, were sold, and the couple relocated to their plantation in Mississippi.

Along the waters of the South Elkhorn Creek in southern Scott County is WEISENBERGER MILL. August Weisenberger, who immigrated to the United States from Baden, Germany, purchased the mill shortly after the Civil War. Today, the mill continues to be operated by the sixth generation of

Ward Hall in Scott County has been described as the "largest Greek Revival house in Kentucky." Construction began in 1853. *Peter Brackney*.

Weisenbergers. The creek serves as the border between Scott County and Woodford County, and the historic Weisenberger Mill site encompasses eighty-seven acres in the two counties.

Finally, the SCOTT COUNTY COURTHOUSE is in itself a landmark, as is the case for many of the courthouses throughout the Commonwealth of Kentucky. Located in the heart of the county seat of Georgetown, the courthouse is located at the corner of East Main and Broadway. Construction began in 1877; it is one of few buildings in the Second Empire style remaining in this region of the country. The location was set aside in 1792 by Reverend Elijah Craig for the first session of the Scott County Court; the present courthouse is the fourth to stand on the site and was constructed after a fire destroyed the third courthouse in 1876. Among the most infamous trials to occur here were those related to the assassination of Kentucky's thirty-fourth governor, William Goebel.

Governor William Goebel had been declared the victor of the 1899 gubernatorial election after the question of the election was decided by the Kentucky legislature. A day before being sworn in, the governor-elect was shot on January 30, 1900, in Frankfort in front of the then-state capitol. Goebel was sworn into office on January 31 and died on February 3. He remains the only U.S. governor to be assassinated while in office. The battle over who would succeed Goebel resulted in much legal maneuvering and found its way to the U.S. Supreme Court. Meanwhile, twenty people were accused of being involved in the assassination. For several of the trials, the venue was changed from Frankfort with the hope that the defendants would receive a fairer trial.

Just as there have been many more trials in the courthouse, there are many more historical places in Scott County (as well as each of the counties included in this book) not included on these pages. The National Register of Historic Places includes eighty-three sites or districts in its registry from Scott County. The county itself was the second created after Kentucky became a state. It was carved out of Woodford County and was named after Virginia native General Charles Scott, who was an officer in the Revolutionary War and served Woodford County in Virginia's legislature. He was also Kentucky's fourth governor, from 1808 to 1812.

BOURBON COUNTY

One of Kentucky's original nine counties, old Bourbon County has been carved into thirty-four of the state's existing counties, including our modern-day Bourbon County. Much of the history of bourbon (the liquor) occurred within old Bourbon County. This geographic area included the Ohio River port community once known as Limestone (now Maysville), where bottles and barrels of bourbon were shipped downriver. The locality name of Bourbon was assigned to the corn-based liquor to quickly distinguish it from other regional mash bills.

(The requirements for bourbon are set forth by federal law in 27 CFR §5.22(b)(1)(i). If you visit any distillery in the region—and you should—you'll likely memorize these as the ABCs of bourbon. All bourbon must be produced in **A**merica or, more specifically, in the United States. The **B**arrel must be of new, charred oak. And the grain mixture must be at least 51 percent **C**orn.)

Some question whether the county is named after bourbon or bourbon is named after the county. The latter is true. The county is named after the House of Bourbon, which is a European royal house founded in 1272. The Bourbons governed France from 1589 until the French Revolution in 1792.

Out of gratitude for Louis XVI's assistance to the American cause in our own revolution, Bourbon County was carved out of Fayette County in 1785.

The county seat of Bourbon County was established at Hopewell, a community renamed in 1790 as Paris (again, honoring the French connection). The Hopewell name survives in the HOPEWELL MUSEUM, the local history and art museum housed in a circa 1910 Beaux-Arts-style post office. It is also the home of the local historical society, HISTORIC PARIS-BOURBON COUNTY (HPBC) and features a Bourbon County History Hall highlighting how the community appeared a century ago. Society members have prepared excellent walking and driving tours through the community's history.

In colonial America, the tavern was an important place for local leaders to gather and discuss the issues of the day. The geographic size of Bourbon County's original borders required people to travel long distances to visit the county seat of Paris to conduct their business. And these individuals needed a place to stay and to eat. Two taverns near the courthouse remain standing. DUNCAN TAVERN, originally called the Goddess of Liberty, was *the* gathering place for Kentucky's earliest leaders, including Daniel Boone,

Built in 1788, Duncan Tavern was an important meeting place for early Kentuckians. Today, it houses the Kentucky Society of the Daughters of the American Revolution. *Peter Brackney*.

Simon Kenton, Peter Houston, and Michael Stoner. Major Joseph Duncan built his inn on the public square in what was then Hopewell, Virginia (now Paris, Kentucky), in 1788 out of locally sourced limestone. It was the first building constructed of stone in the area. According to at least one account, the tavern towered over the twenty-by-thirty-foot log courthouse below. By 1940, the building was dilapidated. It was restored by the Kentucky Society, Daughters of the American Revolution, which now uses the building as its headquarters. Additionally, the KSDAR operates an on-site museum as well as a genealogical library.

Just a few doors down from the Duncan Tavern is Eades Tavern (once Paris's second hotel and now a private residence). It was out of this tavern that postmaster Thomas Eades began operating Paris's first post office in 1795. Robert Trimble both lived and practiced law from this building. In 1826, President John Quincy Adams appointed Trimble to serve on the United States Supreme Court, filling the so-called Kentucky seat on the highest court of the land, continuing a tradition of geographic "diversity" on the bench.

Of course, these taverns were established near the public square because that was the site of the courthouse. As previously noted, the once-sizeable Bourbon County covered about a third of Kentucky. Citizens traveled to the courthouse to litigate their claims, record marriages, and engage in other official business. The courthouse now standing on the public square is the fourth county courthouse on the site and is among the grandest in the state—a far cry from the log structure that once stood below Duncan Tavern. Two major fires, one in 1872 and another in 1901, destroyed both courthouses and some of the county's historic records. Today's grand Bourbon County Courthouse was constructed from 1902 to 1905 at a cost of $170,000. The courthouse was designed by architect Frank P. Milburn of Charleston, South Carolina, to look more like a state capitol than a typical county courthouse. An octagonal "drum" rather than the more traditional circular drum found in many states as well as in Washington is unique to the design, and the interior "is as pretentious yet handsome as the exterior" according to the National Register of Historic Places 1974 nomination form.

One unique relic in the historic courthouse is a window sign above the door to the judge-executive's office proclaiming the space for "Confederates." The room had previously served as a gathering place in the courthouse for Confederate veterans, a space made available during a time that romanticized the South's Lost Cause. Many courthouses in Kentucky had such spaces, including the courthouse in Lexington.

Also on the courthouse square directly across from the Duncan Tavern is a historic marker that recalls the history of McGuffey Readers. A decade before American educator William McGuffey began publishing his infamous readers teaching reading across the country, McGuffey opened a small private school in Paris. The school operated from 1823 until 1826; in 1836, McGuffey began publishing his readers. By 1960, over 120 million copies had been sold. Another historic marker at Tenth and Vine Streets honors a native Parisian, Garrett Morgan. Garrett August Morgan Sr. was born in 1877 to former slaves; his father worked for the local railroad. Garrett left home for Ohio at the age of sixteen. In Cleveland, he developed a dye and tool to help straighten hair. More significantly, however, he received a patent in 1914 for the gas mask, which was sold by his National Safety Device Company. The device was extensively used by Allied forces during World War I. Morgan's most significant and best-known invention, however, was the tri-color traffic light, which he invented after observing the flow of traffic in downtown Cleveland. For this traffic signal, he received a patent

On this site from 1823 until 1826, William McGuffey taught. He began publishing his "readers" a decade later; they would inform millions of Americans until they were discontinued in the 1960s. *Peter Brackney*.

in 1923; thereafter, he sold the rights to his idea to General Electric, which manufactured and sold the device across the nation.

Other downtown Paris buildings are worth note and are included on the previously mentioned walking tour. One in particular is the SHINNER BUILDING at 731 Main Street, which was built around 1891. Edward Shinner had the three-story building constructed; he was the proprietor of a local saloon from 1876 until 1896. After Shinner, a grocer (Lavin and Connell) operated here until the onset of World War I. Upstairs, groups used the large space as event halls. The three-story structure has been described by Ripley's Believe It or Not! as the "tallest three-story building in the world."

A few miles north of Paris is the site of CANE RIDGE MEETING HOUSE. It was the site of the Great Revival of 1801, which began the Protestant Reformation movement in the United States. The meetinghouse is considered America's "most famous" frontier church, and the original 1791 one-room log meetinghouse still stands inside a larger limestone superstructure that was constructed in 1954. The old meetinghouse serves as a museum of church and pioneer history.

CLARK COUNTY

General George Rogers Clark was a Revolutionary War hero and the highest-ranking military officer on the frontier during the conflict leading to victories at Kaskaskia and Vincennes. These victories on the frontier were fodder for General Washington in encouraging the alliance with France that ultimately aided the United States in earning its independence. Five states have a Clark County named after him.

A number of early settlements dotted the landscape, with many of the settlers arriving from the nearby Fort Boonesborough. One of these settlements is being preserved in the LOWER HOWARD'S CREEK STATE NATURE PRESERVE AND HERITAGE PARK, which is publicly accessible via a trailhead near Hall's Restaurant. The natural beauty abounds in this preserve, with approximately four hundred different plant species growing under a canopy of second-growth forest. Unique species include water stitchwort, running buffalo clover, Kentucky viburnum, white walnut, and nodding rattlesnake-root. This now seemingly secluded and isolated valley was once interconnected to the national and global economies through its location on the Kentucky River. Ceramic shards around the significant stone Martin/Bush House (which began as a log cabin in the 1780s) indicated

Ruins of the mill at Lower Howard's Creek in Clark County. *Peter Brackney*.

an unusually high concentration of refined earthenware, evidencing the distant reach of commodities in and out of the Lower Howard's Creek valley. Jonathan Bush likely owned the house (his second wife is buried in a tomb box nearby under an elaborate tablet), and he also owned and operated the nearby mill, which led the area to be economically connected to larger economies via flatboats traveling along the Kentucky River and its tributaries up to the Ohio River and ultimately the Mississippi River toward the city of New Orleans.

Bush's Mill is in such good condition that it is easy to understand how Oliver Evans's automatic flour mill (U.S. Patent No. 3) functioned from what remains of the site. A dam, nearly half a mile upstream from the mill, would have diverted water down the gravity-fed millrace to a point some thirty feet above the mill. A sluice then transported water from this pool to the twenty-foot mill wheel, which turned the mill's numerous inner workings to mill grains into flour.

Throughout the preserve, limestone walls seemingly indigenous to central Kentucky also abound. Many of these have been rebuilt by the Dry Stone Conservancy. Two parallel dry laid limestone walls through a portion of the preserve create a wide path along what would have been part of the old wilderness roads, this portion linking Fort Boonesborough to the Blue Licks.

But as ancient as these ruins might be, the settlers here were by no means the first inhabitants of Clark County. Clovis people first entered Kentucky around 12,000 BCE, spreading across Kentucky from west to east. They arrived in modern-day Clark County about 8500 BCE. Archaic, Adena, and Fort Ancient cultures also extended across the region. By the early eighteenth century, Clark County was the home to one of the most significant Native American communities of the era: the Shawnee town in eastern Clark County called Eskippathiki.

A historic marker identifies the Indian Old Fields as being the site of Eskippathiki, but the precise location is uncertain (though it is thought to have been near the interchange of I-64 and the Mountain Parkway). A French Canadian census conducted in 1736 indicated that the village had a population of two hundred "heads of households," suggesting a total population of between five and eight hundred or more. The site contradicts the misconception that Kentucky was a "dark and bloody ground" uninhabited by Native Americans, though little is known of its history because of limited archaeological discovery.

The city of Winchester is the seat of Clark County and was laid out in 1793 from sixty-six acres donated by frontiersman John Baker. Baker originally hailed from Winchester, Virginia, and named the community after his homeplace. Winchester's Main Street is full of historic sites, though it has not always been so well maintained. As late as 1800, tree stumps still dotted the middle of the roadway, and it was a dirt path until 1910. Today, a walking tour highlights twenty-seven historic places in the downtown area; the tour brochure is available from the Winchester-Clark County Tourism Commission. One of the sites located on the tour is the Bluegrass Heritage Museum in what was once the home and medical office of Dr. Edward P. Guerrant. From this location, Guerrant established a mission clinic and hospital that provided medical care to locals as well as those from the mountains who were not comfortable or could not afford traveling into Lexington. According to the museum, the patients would arrive for care "by mule, stretcher, buckboard, and the Lexington & Eastern Railroad." The museum houses an operating suite and patient room to honor Guerrant and his staff's medical care provided over the course of sixty years, as well as other stories of Bluegrass culture.

Two culinary Kentucky legends arose in Clark County as well. Beer cheese, a sharp cheddar–based spread, originated at the Driftwood Inn on

Winchester's Main Street is an excellent example of an intact commercial district utilizing historic buildings in Central Kentucky. *Peter Brackney*.

the Kentucky River, operated by Johnnie Allman. In the late 1930s, beer cheese and fried banana peppers were served at the Driftwood. The following decade, Allman relocated his restaurant to the site of the present-day HALL'S ON THE RIVER RESTAURANT. Hall's has become a legend in its own right since it opened in 1966. Winchester has capitalized on the increasing popularity of beer cheese with a Beer Cheese Trail as wells as a festival held on the second weekend of June. The other culinary legend is a soft drink bottled in Winchester since 1926: ALE-8-ONE. "A Late One" is the only soft drink to have been invented in Kentucky. George Lee Wainscott began his soft drink company in 1902 and developed a variety of colas, but it was his ginger with citrus combination that became a legend. He first introduced Ale-8-One at the 1926 Clark County Fair, where he held a contest to name the soda. The winning entry ("A Late One") was slang in the 1920s meaning "the latest thing," as Wainscott's recipe was now the latest thing in soft drinks. Traditionally, Ale-8 is sold in glass bottles, and the company describes itself as the oldest glass bottler in the United States.

Winchester and Clark County also have an important place in arts and entertainment history. The LEED'S THEATRE on Main Street was built in

1925 and was one of the first buildings in town to have air conditioning. Now an arts center, it is a model of adaptive reuse in a small community. It was one of the first three theaters in Winchester. The second movie house, the Pastime Theater, operated from 1912 until 1918 when the wall of a burned-out building next door collapsed, killing twelve people who were taking in a movie at the Pastime. A historic marker on Main Street recalls the tragedy and lists the names of the victims. One of the victims was twelve-year-old Tommy Thomas. Tommy's sister, Helen, was born two years after the tragedy.

Helen Thomas was an American journalist and Winchester native who covered the White House during the administrations of ten presidents. Her career in the White House press briefing room began when John F. Kennedy was in the Oval Office, and she retired in 2010 during the administration of Barack Obama. She coined the phrase, "Thank you, Mr. President," and was known also for her quote, "I don't think a tough question is disrespectful."

Another famous native Clark countian was the sculptor Joel T. Hart. He was born in Winchester in 1810 and spent his free time as a youth carving stone and wood for friends. With no formal training, he perfected his trade and moved to Florence, Italy. His best-known works are busts of Andrew Jackson and Henry Clay completed in 1838 and 1847, respectively. One of his greatest works, *Woman Triumphant*, was considered "one of the most perfect masterpieces of sculpture the world has ever known." It was on display in the courthouse in Lexington, Kentucky, but was destroyed in the 1897 fire that consumed that structure. His angel vase sculpture marker bearing "the elegance of a true craftsman and the face of an angel" is described in promotional materials for the Winchester Cemetery.

MADISON COUNTY

One of Kentucky's original settlements was FORT BOONESBOROUGH, today a National Historic Landmark and state historic site. Noted frontiersman Daniel Boone had scouted the area as early as 1769 but established a settlement here on April 1, 1775. Boonesborough was a site of Kentucky firsts as well. It was the site of the first known Christian service to occur in Kentucky; the service was conducted in the Anglican tradition in May 1775. Kentucky's first representative government met here the same month. Within a few short months, four blockhouses and twenty-six cabins constituted Fort Boonesborough.

The Siege of Boonesborough, also known as the Great Siege, occurred in September 1778 during the height of the American Revolution. Daniel Boone had been captured earlier in the year by Shawnee Indians but escaped shortly before the siege to warn his fellow settlers. His trek to Boonesborough took five days and covered 160 miles. The Shawnee, aligned with the British, significantly outnumbered those inside the fort. A siege was laid for ten days before the Shawnees ultimately abandoned the effort to take Boonesborough. Today, a reconstructed working fort gives visitors a glimpse of eighteenth-century life on the frontier.

You can also step back in history by crossing the Kentucky Ferry at Valley View. The VALLEY VIEW FERRY was one of several ferries that crossed the Kentucky River along Madison County, though it is the only one in operation since the 1950s. (Most have been closed altogether or replaced by bridges.) It is accessed in Madison County along the Tates Creek Road; a road of the same name on the other side of the ferry extends all the way into downtown Lexington. On the northern side of the river, the Valley View Ferry comes ashore on the border of Fayette and Jessamine Counties. The original charter for the ferry here was granted to Captain John Craig, a Revolutionary War veteran. The "perpetual and irrevocable" charter was signed by then Virginia governor Patrick Henry at a time when the region was still a part of Virginia. The ferry has continuously operated here, making it the longest continuously operating business in Kentucky.

Colonel John Miller donated fifty acres of land in 1785 for the establishment of a county seat for the newly formed Madison County. The county was named after a Virginia politician, James Madison. Madison was instrumental in the drafting and ratification of the U.S. Constitution; for his efforts, he is known as the Father of the United States Constitution. He also served as the nation's fourth president. Richmond was named after the capital of Virginia, which was the hometown of Colonel Miller. Today, Richmond is the home to EASTERN KENTUCKY UNIVERSITY, which was established by Kentucky's legislature as a normal school for teachers in 1906 as part of an attempt to improve education across Kentucky.

EKU, however, is not the county's oldest institute of higher learning. BEREA COLLEGE was founded in 1855 in southern Madison County. John Gregg Fee, an abolitionist, founded the college on land given to him by Cassius M. Clay. Clay, cousin to Henry Clay, was also opposed to slavery but favored gradual emancipation in lieu of suddenly abolishing slavery. On ten acres, Fee established a town—Berea—named after a biblical town receptive to the gospel. In a one-room schoolhouse, Fee began what would become Berea

The charter for the Valley View Ferry was signed by Virginia's Governor Patrick Henry in 1785. Still in business, it is Kentucky's oldest operating business. *Peter Brackney.*

College, where he proclaimed an anti-slavery gospel a decade before the Civil War. The school was open to both men and women, as well as those of all races. In 1904, Kentucky passed a law that required segregation based on race. Until that time, Berea was the only racially integrated college in Kentucky and in the whole of the southern United States. Berea College challenged the 1904 law but lost its court battle in the U.S. Supreme Court in 1908.

The BOONE TAVERN is owned and operated by Berea College. The hotel and tavern was a spot for travelers to Berea and its college. Among its guests have been Henry Ford, President Calvin Coolidge and Grace Coolidge, Eleanor Roosevelt, Robert Frost, Maya Angelou, and the Dalai Lama. The three-story hotel on the town's main square was built by the college's work programs in 1909. Berea is also well known for its traditional Appalachian arts and crafts, with galleries on the college square as well as the KENTUCKY ARTISAN CENTER closer to the interstate.

Cassius Clay lived in the northern half of Madison County at his home called WHITE HALL. The site is a state historic site managed by Eastern Kentucky University. Cassius was the son of General Green Clay, who fought alongside Daniel Boone in the defense of Boonesborough. The entire family was politically well connected, and Cassius was an early leader in Kentucky's Republican Party. President Lincoln appointed Cassius Clay to serve as the minister to Russia; Clay remained in that post until 1869. During his service to the nation, Clay helped to negotiate the purchase of Alaskan territory from Russia. Clay had a colorful legacy as well.

After his first wife divorced him, Clay (then eighty-four years old) married fifteen-year-old Dora Richardson. By this time, Clay was eccentric and paranoid. He carried with him two pistols and a knife at nearly all times and had a cannon installed inside his home to fire out the front door of White Hall. Some in the local sheriff's office sought to rescue the young girl, thinking that she was married off against her will. It was a good thing her family alerted the authorities that the marriage was, in fact, consensual, as Clay was prepared to use the cannon in defense.

JESSAMINE COUNTY

Jessamine County, Kentucky, is believed to have been named after a settler's daughter, Jessamine Douglass, "who was stealthily tomahawked by an Indian as she rested on the banks of the creek," as it is recalled on the historic marker on the courthouse lawn. It is traditionally believed to be the only Kentucky county to have a feminine name. The county was formed wholly out of Fayette County in 1798; its county seat—Nicholasville—is named after Colonel George Nicholas. Nicholas is considered the author of Kentucky's first constitution in 1792.

Nicholasville was laid out in 1798 as the seat of the new county, but it was not incorporated until 1837. The original town plat was laid out by Reverend John Metcalfe, a friend of Nicholas. Metcalfe's house, built in 1791, still stands on First Street and is considered the oldest residence in Nicholasville.

Another town of significance in Jessamine County is Wilmore, home of ASBURY UNIVERSITY and ASBURY THEOLOGICAL SEMINARY. Asbury was founded in 1890, but its history connects with an older educational institution called Bethel Academy. Bethel was established in 1790 by Bishop Francis Asbury, and John Metcalfe was installed as the first principal; the school was the first Methodist school in Kentucky and the first west of the Appalachian Mountains.

The Thomas Metcalfe House is the oldest house in Nicholasville. *Peter Brackney*.

Wilmore was originally known as "Scott's Station" and was a stop along the Southern Railway route from Cincinnati, Ohio, to Chattanooga, Tennessee. Along the railroad just south of Wilmore stands HIGH BRIDGE. When completed in 1877, the bridge was the tallest above a navigable waterway (the Kentucky River) as well as the world's tallest railroad bridge (275 feet). Work on the bridge had begun over twenty years earlier, but funding and the intervening Civil War prevented completion of the project. A second set of tracks added to the bridge in 1929 significantly altered an original feature from the 1851 work: two stone towers designed by John A. Roebling. Roebling was an American engineer best known for designing the Brooklyn Bridge in New York, but another of his designs (the 1866 John A. Roebling Suspension Bridge connecting Cincinnati, Ohio, and Covington, Kentucky) remains in the commonwealth. A park at High Bridge offers spectacular views of the bridge and a rebuilt Victorian-era pavilion.

While High Bridge was once the tallest bridge, there's also another significant first in Jessamine County. Upstream along the Kentucky River is the location of the first commercial vineyard in the United States. Today, FIRST VINEYARD continues the tradition begun by John James Dufour in

1799. The original commercial vineyard survived only until 1809, when a deep freeze devastated the vines; before this, the wine was sent to Presidents Thomas Jefferson and James Madison. Dufour's original stone terraces were rediscovered in 2006, and six years later First Vineyard reopened. Alexander vines, the original grape used by Dufour, was thought to be extinct, but the current owners of First Vineyard discovered two Alexander vines in the U.S. Department of Agriculture germplasm repository. The repository sent forty cuttings to First Vineyard, and from this, the historic wine tradition continues in southern Jessamine County.

The most significant historic sites in Jessamine County are the CAMP NELSON NATIONAL MONUMENT and the CAMP NELSON NATIONAL CEMETERY. Camp Nelson was established in 1863 as a Union supply depot under the command of Major General Ambrose Burnside. With major transportation lines nearby and a topography that offered natural defenses, the location was ultimately expanded into a major military site encompassing some four thousand acres surrounding an eight-hundred-acre core. Eighty thousand Union troops passed through Camp Nelson, of which ten thousand were African Americans

A soldier's tent during Camp Nelson's Civil War Days held each September. *Peter Brackney*.

who enlisted in the United States Colored Troops (USCT). Camp Nelson was the third-largest USCT recruiting center in the nation.

A dark chapter in Camp Nelson's history occurred in November 1864 when the families of USCT were expelled from the camp amid harsh, freezing conditions. While the law at the time provided a mechanism for freedom for those enlisting, it did not offer such refuge for members of their family. During the expulsion, over one hundred refugees died, creating a national outcry. By January, the military reversed course and offered sanctuary at Camp Nelson once again. In March, Congress emancipated wives, children, and mothers of USCT servicemembers.

The Camp Nelson National Cemetery covers over thirty acres of land that was once part of Camp Nelson. Nearly 2,500 graves date to the Civil War era. Today, over 12,000 members of the armed forces and their families are buried here. Servicemember and veteran funerals at Camp Nelson National Cemetery are unique, as the Camp Nelson Honor Guard, the nation's only volunteer caisson honor guard, provides a horse and caisson and cannon salute. A caisson is a horse-drawn carriage that carries the coffin at a military funeral. Arlington National Cemetery in Virginia and a national cemetery in Texas offer horse-drawn caissons during funerals of servicemembers, but those are offered directly by the military.

BOYLE COUNTY

Danville, the Boyle County seat, could be described as the birthplace of Kentucky. Danville was the first capital of Kentucky before Kentucky was even a state. Kentucky was still a county of Virginia when it became the county seat of Virginia County in 1785. From there, it was established as the center of the Kentucky District of the federal judiciary. From 1784 to 1791, the town hosted ten constitutional conventions to debate and discuss the terms of a state constitution and the terms of separation from Virginia. Kentucky would become the fifteenth state of the Union on June 1, 1792. At Constitution Square State Historic Site, a replica of the courthouse that housed these constitutional conventions stands alongside a replica of the formidable jail that once housed the commonwealth's earliest prisoners. Other structures also exist at this site near downtown Danville, as well as a circle of plaques dedicated to each Kentucky governor.

Across the street from Constitution Square is the McDowell House & Apothecary, which was the home of Dr. Ephraim McDowell. Dr. McDowell's

A replica of the old courthouse in Danville's Constitution Square. In 1792, Kentucky's state constitution was agreed to in the tenth constitutional convention held here. *Peter Brackney*.

father had participated in the multiple constitutional conventions held in the town; the family arrived in 1784. On Christmas morning, 1809, Jane Todd Crawford found herself in Dr. McDowell's home after traveling sixty miles by horseback. Crawford thought she was pregnant, but McDowell instead diagnosed her as having an ovarian tumor. Without anesthesia or antisepsis (neither were then known), McDowell performed the world's first successful ovariotomy, removing a twenty-two-and-a-half-pound tumor. His patient went on to live another thirty-two years; McDowell became known as the Father of Abdominal Surgery.

As well as being a City of Firsts, Danville (population approximately 16,800) has served a super-sized role in developing American leaders. President Woodrow Wilson, in speaking to alumna of Princeton, said of Danville's CENTRE COLLEGE that "there is a little college town in Kentucky which… has graduated more men who have acquired prominence and fame than has Princeton in her 150 years." Among the notable alum of Centre College are a chief justice of the United States Supreme Court (Fred M. Vinson), an associate justice (John Marshall Harlan) and two vice presidents (John C. Breckinridge and Adlai E. Stevenson), as well as thirteen U.S. senators, eleven governors, and forty-three members of Congress. Additionally, in both 2000 and again in 2012, Centre College hosted the vice-presidential debates. The original campus building, Old Centre, remains; it was constructed in 1819 and is believed to be the oldest college building in the South.

During the Civil War, Old Centre was utilized as a hospital following the Battle of Perryville, which occurred on October 8, 1862. The battle was the last serious attempt by Confederate forces to gain Kentucky. For the Union, Kentucky was important, as it was a slave state that did not secede, its position on the Ohio River was strategically critical, and it was personally important to Kentucky native Abraham Lincoln. Of Kentucky, Lincoln once said, "I hope to have God on my side, but I must have Kentucky."

The Battle of Perryville was the largest conflict in Kentucky during the Civil War. Perryville, just ten miles from Danville, witnessed nearly 7,500 casualties during the battle, which has been considered by some historians as a turning point in the war. Today, the Battle of Perryville State Historic Site has preserved nearly 750 acres of battlefield. Because so much of the land remains as it did in the 1860s, the site is considered one of the nation's great Civil War sites to visit.

MERCER COUNTY

Harrodsburg was Kentucky's first chartered city, established in 1785 by the Virginia legislature. The region was part of Kentucky County, Virginia. Mercer County was created out of Lincoln County in 1780. The early importance of the area was due to Fort Harrod, which was the first permanent settlement in Kentucky. A reconstruction of the fort stands at Old Fort Harrod State Park. This early settlement was led by James Harrod and thirty-one others who first settled here in June 1774. Raids by Native Americans, however, prompted the settlers to abandon the site until the following spring. The reconstructed fort opened in 1927, and a monument honoring the first permanent settlement west of the Allegheny Mountains was dedicated here by President Franklin D. Roosevelt in 1934. Also on the grounds of the park are a pioneer cemetery, a restored 1813 mansion with a collection of artifacts from the fifteenth through the twentieth centuries, and the Lincoln Marriage Temple: Abraham Lincoln's parents were married in Mercer County.

A reenactor prepares to shoot a musket outside Fort Harrod in Harrodsburg, Kentucky. *Peter Brackney*.

The Fort Harrod State Park is on College Street in Harrodsburg, not far from the city center. A ten-minute walk south lies the BEAUMONT INN, which has served Kentucky hospitality for five generations of innkeeping. Today, the Beaumont Inn is described as Kentucky's oldest southern country inn. It opened in 1919 on grounds that had once served as the Greenville Springs Spa and was the childhood home of Chief Justice John Harlan of the U.S. Supreme Court. The Main Inn building was built in 1845 as a women's college; two other buildings constructed in the 1930s also provide rooms at the inn. Throughout the hotel are artifacts and images of local and regional Kentucky history.

Between the Beaumont Inn and the center of Harrodsburg's historic downtown are many pre–Civil War homes of various architectural styles, including Greek Revival, Beaux-Arts, and Queen Anne. The Old Mercer County Jail on South Chiles Street once housed Lizzie Hardin, a Confederate sympathizer who waved her kerchief at General John Hunt Morgan, the Southern general who led guerrilla-style raids, including one near Harrodsburg in 1862. Eighty-five sites are noted on the HARRODSBURG

Walking and Driving Tour, which is better experienced mostly on foot. The guide is available at most local venues, as well as from the Harrodsburg/Mercer County Tourist Commission.

With over three thousand acres, the largest historical destination in Mercer County was home to the third-largest Shaker community in the United States. Living here from 1805 to 1910, members of the religious order pursued a simple life. The Christian sect organized in England before coming to the United States in the 1780s; their faith was noted for its pacifism, equality, and celibacy. Shaker Village of Pleasant Hill began as a poor community but grew in prosperity as its produce and wares commanded a higher price for their quality. At the community's height, the Shakers constructed more than 260 structures on site, of which 34 remain. In addition to the historic center of Shakertown, many acres can be hiked through reestablished native ecosystems. The Shakertown property touches the Kentucky River, and Shaker Landing is one of the few landing points in the Kentucky River Palisades exposing rock formations between 400 and 500 million years old. The old 1826 roadbed can be

Restoration of the Centre Family Dwelling at Shaker Village of Pleasant Hill, which once housed eighty Shakers in fourteen bedrooms. *Peter Brackney*.

hiked today; it was utilized to connect the Shakertown economy to the rivers of the Kentucky, Ohio, and Mississippi, allowing for trading to New Orleans and beyond.

At the landing you can also ride on the *Dixie Belle*, a 115-passenger paddle wheeler, which features narrated cruises that explore the river's historic magnitude. The paddle wheeler also carries its passengers under the High Bridge, the 1877 landmark discussed in the Jessamine County section of this book.

WOODFORD COUNTY

Some of the most famous horse farms in the world are located in Woodford County: Aidrie Stud, Three Chimneys, Lane's End, and many more. Queen Elizabeth II has visited Kentucky five times and generally opts to stay at LANE'S END FARM, owned by William and Sarah Farrish. William Farrish served as the U.S. ambassador to Great Britain during the first administration of President George W. Bush. The Farrishes established Lane's End in 1979, and it is one of many horse farms and equine-related operations you can visit in Woodford County (and elsewhere throughout the Bluegrass). HORSE COUNTRY INC. organizes tours of many of these sites and shares the experience of Kentucky's rich equine heritage; other equine farms and facilities offer independent tours.

Of course, one of Kentucky's other signature industries is bourbon. And Woodford County is home to one of Kentucky's oldest distilleries: WOODFORD RESERVE. Distillation began at the Glenn's Creek site in 1812, when Elijah Pepper began his operation on his newly acquired farm. For the Pepper family, bourbon was a family tradition. Elijah Pepper's son, Colonel James E. Pepper, started the recently restored distillery in Lexington that has become the centerpiece of the Distillery District. In 1878, the Pepper family sold the distillery to Leopold Labrot and James Graham, for whom the distillery is also historically named (Labrot & Graham's Old Oscar Pepper Distillery). Today, the property is under the Brown-Forman label as it has been off and on since 1941. Most of the production process at Woodford Reserve occurs inside a limestone building that was constructed in 1838 by the Pepper family. As with many distilleries throughout the commonwealth, history is rich at Woodford Reserve.

There are two primary communities in Woodford County: Versailles and Midway. The former is pronounced *ver-SALES* and not *ver-SIGH*, so it should not be confused with the French palace. On the road between Lexington and Versailles, however, stands another castle. Originally begun by developer as a gift to his wife in 1969, the castle remained unfinished until the 2000s. For decades, the landmark Kentucky Castle was a roadside tourist destination and photo opportunity in the bygone area of roadside attractions. Restored, it has served as a hotel and event venue. Although the main structure has only just reached the half-century mark in age, the site has a much older vibe given its European inspiration.

The Kentucky Castle is also just around the corner from the Pisgah Presbyterian Church (founded in 1784). Among the historic congregants of this church was Albert Benjamin "Happy" Chandler, who served as a two-term governor of Kentucky. The medical center at the University of Kentucky is named in his honor, as he was instrumental in its establishment. He also served as the national baseball commissioner. In that role, Chandler approved Jackie Robinson paving the way for desegregation of major-league baseball.

The community of Midway is so named because it is located at the midpoint between Lexington and the state capital, Frankfort. For this reason,

Located midway between Frankfort and Lexington, Midway, Kentucky, features many shops and restaurants on either side of its historic Main Street. The old railroad tracks go down the middle of the road. *Peter Brackney*.

the railroad town of Stevenson (later Middleway) assumed its current moniker in 1837. Two years earlier, the land that became Midway was purchased by the Lexington & Ohio Railroad Company, becoming the first Kentucky town established by a railroad. Today, Midway's historic Main Street is filled with restaurants and shops in historic nineteenth-century commercial buildings. Down the middle of Main Street, set apart from vehicular and pedestrian traffic, are the still-active railroad tracks that gave birth to this community nearly two centuries ago.

Henry Wadsworth Longfellow's poem forever memorialized the midnight ride of Paul Revere, but Revere was not the only Patriot during the Revolutionary War to take an overnight ride for the cause of freedom. Captain John "Jack" Jouett Jr. made such a ride through central Virginia on the night of June 3–4, 1781. Some 250 British regulars were descending on Charlottesville, where they would seek to capture or kill political prisoners like Virginia's then-governor Thomas Jefferson as well as the members of the Virginia legislature. His ride saved many early leaders in the American cause. After the war, Jouett located across the mountains and settled here with his wife at the JACK JOUETT HOUSE. The couple had twelve children, among them the noted portrait painter Matthew Harris Jouett. Jouett House tours include a 1780s stone cabin and the Federal-style brick home built by the Jouetts.

FRANKLIN COUNTY

The state capitol is located in Frankfort and with it a rich history. The Beaux-Arts design was completed in 1910. When it was built, the KENTUCKY STATE CAPITOL was the tallest building in Kentucky at 210 feet. Under the rotunda are four murals representing agriculture, industry, civilization, and integrity. The murals were part of the original capitol design but were not completed until the centennial celebration in 2010. The original artist for the murals was to be Frank Millet, who was a friend of then-governor August E. Stanley. Millet, however, died on the ill-fated maiden voyage of the *Titanic* in 1912, and the mural project was abandoned for nearly a century. Beneath the murals lies a statuary hall, where Kentucky native Abraham Lincoln takes center stage. The sixteenth president is surrounded by three other Kentuckians: Dr. Ephraim McDowell (see Boyle County), the "Great Compromiser" Henry Clay, and former vice president Alben Barkley. From 1936 until 2020, a statue of Confederate president Jefferson Davis stood in

The Kentucky State Capitol in Frankfort was completed in 1910. When completed, it was the tallest building in the commonwealth. *Peter Brackney*.

the prominent rotunda before being removed by a state commission; a statue of another Kentuckian will likely be added to the rotunda at a later date.

A statewide debate preceded the construction of the new capitol, with Louisville, Lexington, and Frankfort bidding to be the state capital. The existing capitol building, which remains standing in old Frankfort, had become too small to accommodate the state government. Obviously, Frankfort won the debate and remained the capital.

The GOVERNOR'S MANSION also stands on the capitol grounds. It has been the state executive's home since 1914. Like the neighboring capitol, the Governor's Mansion is in the Beaux-Arts design and was modeled after Queen Marie Antoinette's summer villa Petit Trianon. Governor Wilson suggested the need for an executive residence closer to the capitol the year after the new capitol was built, but it was his successor who first occupied the residence.

Both the capitol and the Governor's Mansion are located in "new" Frankfort on the south side of the Kentucky River. Across the Singing Bridge is "old" Frankfort. The prior governor's mansion and the old capitol both still stand in old Frankfort. Singing Bridge is a Pennsylvania truss design

The Governor's Mansion is designed after Marie Antoinette's summer villa, Le Petite Trianon, in Versailles, France. *Peter Brackney*.

with a steel deck; as cars travel across the deck, the humming sound gives the circa 1893 bridge its name. Once the longest single-span structure in Kentucky, the current "singing" floor was installed in 1938.

Over in old Frankfort, governors had occupied the OLD GOVERNOR'S MANSION since it was built in 1796. This Georgian-style residence was nearer the old capitol in old Frankfort. Today, it officially serves as the residence of the lieutenant governor, though it has not been officially occupied for over a decade. It remains open for tours to visitors. James Garrard, Kentucky's second governor, was the first to occupy the building. Two later occupant-governors, Thomas Metcalfe and Robert P. Letcher, had been craftsmen working on the building's construction.

Just two blocks away stands the OLD STATE CAPITOL, which served as Kentucky's capitol from 1830 until the completion of the new capitol in 1910. A native Kentucky architect, Gideon Shryock, designed the Greek Revival building. The façade's six columns are topped by marble pediments. An iconic cupola tops the building, allowing for natural light and ventilation into the structure. Inside, the double self-supporting staircase impresses

Singing Bridge in Frankfort was built in 1893. The current floor, installed in 1938, sings when cars cross. *Peter Brackney*.

given the design and construction in the first half of the nineteenth century. The Old State Capitol was constructed of locally quarried Kentucky River marble, also known as limestone. Laborers from the old state penitentiary, which was then directly across the street from the Old Governor's Mansion, cut the stone.

On the lawn of the Old State Capitol is a statue honoring the only governor in the country to have died from an assassin's bullet while in office. Governor-elect William Goebel was walking to the old capitol on January 30, 1900, when an assassin's bullet struck him in the chest. Kentucky's legislature had just decided the close election in his favor, reversing the popular vote. Wounded, Goebel was sworn into office on his deathbed. Succession was disputed and ultimately decided in the courts, the case of *Taylor v. Beckham* rising to the United States Supreme Court.

A statue of William Goebel, as well as this plaque, are located on the grounds of the Old State Capitol, where Goebel was fatally shot on January 30, 1900. He would be sworn in as Kentucky's thirty-fourth governor on his deathbed. *Peter Brackney.*

Close to the Old Capitol is the THOMAS D. CLARK CENTER FOR KENTUCKY HISTORY, where history lovers can discover more about the past twelve thousand years of Kentucky's history. The center also contains the state's genealogical research library and a Hall of Governors to discover the stories of Kentucky's executives. The center is operated by the Kentucky Historical Society, which was established in 1836 to preserve and protect the legacy of Kentucky. The Kentucky Historical Society operates the Old State Capitol, and tours begin at the center. KHS also operates the KENTUCKY MILITARY HISTORY MUSEUM, which is located on East Main Street in the old state arsenal. The military museum contains weapons exhibits and highlights Kentuckians who fought for the United States throughout our nation's history.

Frankfort's CAPITAL CITY MUSEUM is located at the site of the old Capital Hotel, which is where the wounded Goebel was brought after he was shot. An exhibit re-creates the scene on the site where Dr. Hume attempted to save his life. The museum contains other exhibits, both permanent and rotating, that tell the two-hundred-plus-year story of Kentucky's capital city. The museum also serves as a starting point for several downtown walking tours.

Because of Frankfort's status as Kentucky's capital, it is impossible to quickly tell the importance of its many places. The Downtown Frankfort Walking Tour helps your feet walk through history to see homes incredible to Kentucky and America's history. This includes the home where Bibb lettuce was first cultivated (Bibb-Burnley House). Liberty Hall was the home of Kentucky's first senator (John Brown) and a place where President James Monroe dined alongside future presidents Zachary Taylor and Andrew Jackson. Other famous (or infamous) visitors included General Marquis de Lafayette and Aaron Burr. John Brown had another home constructed in 1835 by Gideon Shryock, and it is one of only a few residences designed by this important Kentucky architect. A celebrity row of houses connects to the many supreme court justices who hailed from Kentucky, including John Marshall Harlan and Thomas Todd, as well as Kentucky governors and senators and judges. At the corner of Broadway and Washington Streets was the home of Francis Preston Blair Jr., who is better known for his Blair House in Washington, D.C. Dubbed the "President's Guest House," Blair House has housed countless dignitaries and is traditionally where the president-elect stays leading up to inauguration. The walking tour and driving tour brochures can be obtained at various sites throughout town as well as at the Frankfort Tourist Commission offices.

A historic visit to Frankfort would not be complete without honoring those buried at the Frankfort Cemetery. Seventeen Kentucky governors and many other distinguished souls are buried here. Two of the cemetery's most notable residents are pioneer Daniel Boone and his wife, Rebecca. Although Boone's story is Kentucky's settlement story, Boone died in Missouri in 1820 and was buried there. The Frankfort Cemetery, established in 1844, became the new final resting place for the Boones' bodies after they were disinterred and transported here in 1845. Or so we believe. There is some dispute on whether the correct remains were removed from Missouri. Located on a bluff on the south side of the Kentucky River, the cemetery also offers incredible views of the capital city below.

The oldest continually operating distillery in the United States is the Buffalo Trace Distillery. Bourbon operations began on this site as early as 1775. The first distillery was constructed by Harrison Blanton in 1812, and it was purchased by E.H. Taylor in 1870. George T. Stagg purchased the operation in 1878. For bourbon drinkers, these historic names are all labels produced on site. During America's prohibition experiment, the distillery remained operational for "medicinal purposes." The gorgeous distillery sits on 440 acres and offers a variety of different tours. History

A rickhouse at Buffalo Trace Distillery, the oldest bourbon distillery in Kentucky. A rickhouse is where bourbon ages in oak barrels for at least four years (as required by law). *Peter Brackney.*

lovers may particularly enjoy the National Historic Landmark Tour that focuses on the buildings, architecture, and history of 1933–53 (the period of significance for which the historic landmark distinction is based).

7

WHAT'S OUTSIDE MY HOTEL WINDOW?

The view outside a hotel room depends on the building orientation and the side of the building a room faces. This chapter gives a quick description of the historic buildings, sites, and features visible from the principal hotels in Lexington. Some of the historic features mentioned are described in more detail elsewhere in this book.

A word about Lexington's compass orientation. While it is common to refer to West Main and South Mill Streets, for example, the orientation is more northeast–southwest than true north–south. This is due to the pioneer street pattern lining up along the Town Branch of the Elkhorn River, which used to run through the center of the town and is now under Vine Street. The local version of north will be used here.

HYATT REGENCY

The Hyatt faces High (formerly Hill) Street, named for its elevation above the new village of Lexington. Looking north, the hotel overlooks Triangle Park and the Victorian-era commercial block of buildings, at this printing called The Square. It was called Victorian Square when the block was renovated from warehouse and ground floor retail into a mixed-use shopping mall, restaurants, and offices. Over and to the west of the Square lies a local historic district (the Western Suburb) and two historic churches (St. Paul's Catholic Church and First Baptist Church). If a room is high enough, the top of Lexington's 1882 Opera House can be seen. To the west, over the tree canopy of the Lexington Cemetery, the statue of Henry Clay that stands over his and his wife's grave is visible.

To the south, past the surface parking lots, Historic Pleasant Green Baptist Church faces the hotel. Along Broadway, running past the movie theaters and parking garage, is the site of one of the earliest racetracks in Lexington. To the left or east of Broadway is the South Hill Historic District.

HILTON

The Hilton sits at right angles to the Hyatt and thus is afforded different views. The view to the west along Broadway oversees Triangle Park, formerly the site of a flour mill and warehouses. The Square, a collection of Victorian-era commercial buildings, now a mixed-use mall, is to the north of the park. In the distance, over the tree canopy of the Lexington Cemetery, stands the statue of Henry Clay. The statue is atop a column and monument over the graves of Clay and his wife, Lucretia. Depending on which end of the hotel a room is located, the childhood home of Mary Todd Lincoln, the wife of the president, is visible.

The view from rooms facing east, unfortunately, show little. The office building on the other side of the parking garage sits on the site of the first settlement of Lexington, a fortified station of three rows of cabins connected by log walls to protect against Indian attacks. Some rooms can see, at an angle, the restored historic Old Courthouse.

21C

Hotel 21C is itself a historic building. It was the first skyscraper in Lexington and home, on the ground floor, of one of its major banks, the First National Bank. To longtime residents, it is still called the First National Building.

On the south or Main Street side, the primary historic building in view is the Melodeon Building. In the nineteenth century, a major theater was on the second floor. Abraham and Mary Todd Lincoln once attended a play at the Melodeon. That upper space has been divided horizontally into two floors of offices.

The view to the west is dramatic, looking across Upper Street at the restored 1899 Historic Courthouse. The VisitLEX Visitor's Center in

Old Morrison, on the campus of Transylvania University, has a crypt containing the remains of a professor who cursed the university. The curse was followed by multiple fires, which destroyed parts of campus. *Peter Brackney*.

located on the near ground floor corner. On the other side of the courthouse is Cheapside Park, long the center of the town market house, county court days, and slave auctions.

Two blocks to the north are visible the treetops of historic Gratz Park, a local historic district. Just north of the Park is Transylvania University, and if the room is high enough, its long revered Old Morrison building is visible.

The eastern view looks down Main Street toward, to the south, the treed neighborhood of Ashland Park, subdivided out of Henry Clay's farm. Lost in the trees is Ashland, Henry Clay's home. Near Ashland, the road becomes divided by parkway medians. The medians were created as a result of that strip of road being the speedway for carriage races running east, turning at the end of the parks, and coming down the "home stretch" back toward town. A stone monument recognizes the speedway.

RESIDENCE INN DOWNTOWN

The view northmost immediately is the 21C Hotel, located in Lexington's first skyscraper. To the northwest is the historic Old Courthouse, erected in 1899, and Cheapside Park, long site of the local market houses, court day trading days, political rallies, and slave auctions.

West of the hotel is the Melodeon Theater building, the site of a major theater on the second floor during the nineteenth century. There are no historic views to the south or east.

J.W. MARRIOTT

Southern windows principally show the Vine Street corridor of modern twentieth-century buildings, but just up the hill to High Street is the South Hill Historic District. On the corner at Limestone and Vine Streets is a small two-story building that once housed Henry Clay's favorite tavern.

THE SIRE HOTEL

The Sire is located on the edge of the Gratz Park Historic District, and the views to the north and northwest are of historic houses, many now converted to offices. Directly north, across Second Street, is the Abraham Barton house, the earliest part of which dates to the early 1800s. It originally faced Second, but later additions reoriented the building to face Upper Street. Views to the west show the rear of old commercial buildings along Limestone and the history Sayre School, begun as a women's college in the 1800s.

Columbia's Steakhouse on North Limestone opened in 1948 and is Lexington's oldest restaurant. *Peter Brackney*.

MARRIOTT GRIFFIN GATE AND EMBASSY SUITES

These are treated together, as they share a view. The Marriott faces across Newtown Pike, and the Embassy Suites is located on the former McGrathania Stud Farm. Hal Price McGrath owned a gambling house in New York City and made enough profit to buy the horse farm. On this farm, he bred Aristides, the horse that won the very first Kentucky Derby. After McGrath's death, the farm was purchase by Colonel Milton Young, who made it into one of the most famous Thoroughbred breeding operations in the country. Among his sires was the great Thoroughbred Hanover. Later, Chicago oil baron C.B. Shaffer bought the farm, added more acreage, and changed its name to Coldstream Farm. In 1957, the farm was acquired by the University of Kentucky for use by the College of Agricultural. In 1982, it was converted to an office and research park by the university.

BEAUMONT-AREA HOTELS

Famous horseman Hal Price Headley owned Beaumont Farm, a four-thousand-plus-acre Thoroughbred horse farm that produced many winning horses, including Kentucky Oaks winner Alcibiades. He was a co-founder of Keeneland Race Course. Most of the farm has been developed into housing, shopping areas, office developments, and hotels.

RESIDENCE INN ON SOUTH BROADWAY

The Residence Inn on South Broadway, along with the surrounding developments, was constructed on former tobacco warehouse property dating from the days when Lexington held the largest burley tobacco sales in the world. Outside the rear room windows is an excellent view of the Red Mile, a standardbred trotting track dating to 1875. To the left, as viewed from the inn, is the famous Floral Barn or Round Barn, built in 1882 and used first as an exhibition hall to display floral arrangement contests during fairs. It now houses the Standardbred Stable of Memories.

RESOURCES

BOURBON COUNTY RESOURCES

CANE RIDGE MEETING HOUSE
1655 Cane Ridge Road, Paris
(859) 987-5350
www.caneridge.org

DUNCAN TAVERN HISTORIC CENTER
323 High Street, Paris
(859) 987-1788
www.duncantavern.com

HISTORIC PARIS–BOURBON COUNTY/HOPEWELL MUSEUM
800 Pleasant Street, Paris
(859) 987-7274
www.hopewellmuseum.org

BOYLE COUNTY RESOURCES

CENTRE COLLEGE
600 West Walnut Street, Danville
(859) 238-5200
www.centre.edu

Constitution Square State Historic Site
105 East Walnut Street, Danville
kentuckytourism.com/constitution-square-historic-site

Danville-Boyle County Visitors Bureau
105 East Walnut Street, Danville
(859) 236-7794
www.visitdanvilleky.com

McDowell House & Apothecary
125 South Second Street, Danville
(859) 236-2804
www.mcdowellhouse.com

Perryville Battlefield State Historic Site
1825 Battlefield Road, Perryville
(859) 332-8631
parks.ky.gov/perryville/parks/historic/perryville-battlefield-state-historic-site

CLARK COUNTY RESOURCES

Ale-8-One
25 Carol Road, Winchester
(859) 744-3484
www.ale8one.com

Bluegrass Heritage Museum
217 South Main Street, Winchester
(859) 745-1358
www.bgheritage.com

Hall's on the River
1225 Athens Boonesboro Road, Winchester
(859) 527-6620

Lower Howard's Creek State Natural Preserve and Heritage Park
1225 Athens Boonesboro Road, Winchester
(859) 744-4888
www.lowerhowardscreek.org

WINCHESTER CEMETERY
625 West Lexington Avenue, Winchester
(859) 744-0556

WINCHESTER-CLARK COUNTY TOURISM COMMISSION
2 South Maple Street, Winchester
(859) 744-0556
www.tourwinchester.com

FAYETTE COUNTY

BLUE GRASS TRUST FOR HISTORIC PRESERVATION
210 North Broadway, Lexington
(859) 253-0362
www.bluegrasstrust.org

LEXINGTON CEMETERY
833 West Main Street, Lexington
(859) 255-5522
www.lexcem.org

LEXINGTON HISTORY MUSEUM
317 South Mill Street, Lexington
(859) 721-5678
www.lexhistory.org

LEXINGTON PUBLIC LIBRARY
140 East Main Street, Lexington
(859) 231-5500
www.lexpublib.org

TRANSYLVANIA UNIVERSITY
300 North Broadway, Lexington
(859) 233-8797
www.transy.edu

UNIVERSITY OF KENTUCKY
100 Funkhouser Building, Lexington
(859) 562-2287
www.uky.edu

VisitLex
215 West Main Street #150, Lexington
859-233-1221
www.visitlex.com

FRANKLIN COUNTY

Buffalo Trace Distillery
113 Great Buffalo Trace, Frankfort
(502) 696-5926
www.buffalotracedistillery.com

Frankfort Cemetery
215 East Main Street, Frankfort
(502) 227-2403
www.frankfortcemetery.org

Frankfort Tourist Commission
100 Capital Avenue, Frankfort
(800) 960-7200
www.visitfrankfort.com

Governor's Mansion
704 Capitol Avenue, Frankfort
(502) 564-3449
governorsmansion.ky.gov

Kentucky Historical Society
100 West Broadway Street, Frankfort
(502) 564-1792
www.history.ky.gov

Kentucky State Capitol
700 Capitol Ave., Frankfort
(502) 564-3449
historicproperties.ky.gov/hp/ncs/

Old Governor's Mansion
420 High Street, Frankfort
(502) 564-3449
historicproperties.ky.gov/np/ogm/

JESSAMINE COUNTY RESOURCES

Asbury University & Theological Seminary
1 Macklem Drive, Wilmore
(859) 858-3511
www.asbury.edu

Camp Nelson National Monument
6614 Old Danville Road, Loop 2, Nicholasville
(859) 881-5716
www.nps.gov/cane

First Vineyard
5800 Sugar Creek Pike, Nicholasville
(859) 885-9359
www.firstvineyard.net

High Bridge Park
KY 29 and Old Park Road, Wilmore
(859) 885-4500

Jessamine County Tourism Commission
102 South First Street, Nicholasville
(859) 305-6040
www.visitjessamine.com

MADISON COUNTY RESOURCES

BEREA COLLEGE
101 Chestnut Street, Berea
(859) 985-3000
www.berea.edu

FORT BOONESBOROUGH STATE PARK
4375 Boonesborough Road, Richmond
(859) 527-3131
parks.ky.gov

VALLEY VIEW FERRY
(from Richmond, take KY 169 N)
(from Nicholasville, take KY 169 S)
(from Lexington, take KY 1974 S)
Operating Status information via
www.lexingtonky.gov/valley-view-ferry

WHITE HALL HISTORIC SITE
500 White Hall Shrine Road, Richmond
(859) 623-9178
parks.ky.gov

MERCER COUNTY RESOURCES

BEAUMONT INN
638 Beaumont Inn Dr., Harrodsburg
(859) 734-3381
www.beaumontinn.com

FORT HARROD STATE PARK
100 South College Street, Harrodsburg
(859) 734-3314
parks.ky.gov/Harrodsburg/parks/historic/old-fort-harrod-state-park

HARRODSBURG/MERCER COUNTY TOURIST COMMISSION
488 Price Avenue, Harrodsburg
(859) 734-2364
www.harrodsburgky.com

SCOTT COUNTY RESOURCES

Georgetown/Scott County Information Center
399 Outlet Center Drive, Georgetown
(888) 863-8600
www.GeorgetownKY.com

Georgetown Scott County Museum
229 East Main Street, Georgetown
(502) 863-6201
www.georgetownscottcountymuseum.com

Toyota Visitors Center
1001 Cherry Blossom Way, Georgetown
(800) 866-4485
www.tourtoyota.com/kentucky

Ward Hall Preservation Foundation, Inc.
1782 Frankfort Road, Georgetown
(502) 863-5356
www.wardhall.net

Weisenberger Mill
2545 Weisenberger Mill Road, Midway
(859) 254-5282
www.weisenberger.com

Yuko-En on the Elkhorn
400 East College Street, Georgetown
(502) 316-4554
www.yuko-en.com

WOODFORD COUNTY RESOURCES

Horse Country, Inc.
(859) 963-1004
www.visithorsecountry.com

Jack Jouett House
225 Craig's Creek Road, Versailles
(859) 873-7902
www.jouetthouse.org

Kentucky Castle
230 Pisgah Pike, Versailles
(859) 256-0322
thekentuckycastle.com

Pisgah Presbyterian Church
710 Pisgah Pike, Versailles
(859) 873-4161
www.pisgahchurch.org

Woodford Reserve Distillery
7785 McCracken Pike, Versailles
(859) 879-1812
www.woodfordreserve.com

INDEX

ABOUT THE AUTHORS

PETER BRACKNEY is an attorney who practices bankruptcy, estate planning, and probate law in his adopted hometown of Lexington, Kentucky. He is a double alumnus of the University of Kentucky and has served on the boards of different local history and historic preservation organizations. He has previously written *Lost Lexington*, which chronicled the backstories of Lexington's landmarks that have been lost to history, and *The Murder of Geneva Hardman and Lexington's Mob Riot of 1920*, which delves into a dark chapter in central Kentucky's history. He has blogged since 2009 at www.thekaintuckeean. com and lives in Jessamine County with his wife and three children.

FOSTER OCKERMAN JR., a Lexington native and seventh-generation Kentuckian, is a historian as well as a practicing attorney. A graduate of the University of North Carolina (1974, American history) and the University of Kentucky College of Law (1977), he has represented or served on the boards of numerous nonprofits and foundations at the local, state and national levels. He is a founding trustee of the Lexington History Museum Inc. He now serves the museum as president and chief historian. He was named the Outstanding Citizen Lawyer by the Fayette County Bar Association in 2018. He is also a former rock-and-roll disk jockey and a retired professional soccer referee. Ockerman is the author of five works of history, including *Historic Lexington*, the most recent history of Lexington, Kentucky; an anthology of his poetry; and *The Ockerman Genealogical Project*, as well as numerous opinion essays. His most recent book, *The Hidden History of Horse Racing*, was published by The History Press in March 2019. He was also historian for the Emmy Award–winning documentary *Belle Brezing*. Foster is married to Reverend Martina Y. Ockerman (United Methodist Church). They have two daughters and two grandchildren.